The Rise of the Equalities Industry

The Rise of the Equalities Industry

Peter Saunders

Civitas: Institute for the Study of Civil Society
London

First Published November 2011

© Civitas 2011
55 Tufton Street
London SW1P 3QL

email: books@civitas.org.uk

ISBN 978-1-906837-33-4

Independence: Civitas: Institute for the Study of Civil Society is a registered educational charity (No. 1085494) and a company limited by guarantee (No. 04023541). Civitas is financed from a variety of private sources to avoid over-reliance on any single or small group of donors.

All publications are independently refereed. All the Institute's publications seek to further its objective of promoting the advancement of learning. The views expressed are those of the authors, not of the Institute.

Typeset by
Civitas

Printed in Great Britain by

Berforts Group Ltd
Stevenage SG1 2BH

Contents

Acknowledgements

Many thanks to Tej Nathwani who worked as an intern at Civitas in the Summer of 2010 and collected much invaluable material for this project. I am also grateful to the staff in the Primary Care Trusts and County Councils who provided details of their equality and diversity budgets. Robert Greig offered useful advice on gender pay-gap statistics, David Harrison helped think through some issues, and David Green was a constant source of support and inspiration. Three anonymous referees provided very useful critiques and feedback which helped to strengthen the analysis.

.

Author

Peter Saunders is a Professorial Fellow of Civitas, and author of *Social Mobility Myths*, published by Civitas in 2010. Until 1999, he was Professor of Sociology at the University of Sussex, where he is still Professor Emeritus, and he has held visiting academic posts at universities in Australia, Germany, New Zealand and the United States. After 1999, he worked as Research Manager at the Australian Institute of Family Studies, and as Social Research Director at the Centre for Independent Studies in Sydney, where he remains a Distinguished Fellow. In 2008 he returned to the UK where he is an independent writer and consultant. In addition to his work for Civitas, his publications include *A Nation of Home Owners; Capitalism — A Social Audit; Social Theory and the Urban Question; Introduction to British Politics; Privatisation and Popular Capitalism, Australia's welfare habit and how to kick it* and, most recently, *When Prophecy Fails*. More details of his work can be found at www.petersaunders.org.uk.

Foreword

When democracy is at its best, political parties compete by offering alternative visions of the common good. But competition for votes can easily be distorted into a bidding war between parties who buy the support of significant voting blocs. One of the most pernicious developments in recent times has been the practice of offering preferential treatment to collections of individuals who claim a group identity, often based on race or religion.

The key to gaining political recognition of entitlement to preferential treatment is to be acknowledged as a victim. The disadvantage of this culture of victimhood is that we have become less concerned with the common good, hoping to provide opportunities for everyone to fulfil their potential. Instead, we have become more like a society made up of groups with grievances trying to gain advantage at the expense of the others.

A major problem for victim groups is that once they have been given preferential treatment their power increases, thus undermining their case for special treatment. Consequently, groups intent on maintaining their victim status have made strenuous efforts to invent and nurse grievances. Highlighting historic wrongs such as slavery has proved especially appealing because it involves harvesting sympathy for suffering by other people a long while ago. For today's victim-groups it is zero-cost victimhood. Falsely claiming to have been 'insulted' is another painless tool. An important part of this strategy requires establishing the victim as the sole judge of when language is hurtful. To keep alleged oppressors on the defensive, the words that cause offence are changed from time to time. Recently the commonly-used term 'mental handicap' was redefined as insulting. And Stonewall in Wales decided that the term 'openly gay' was a term of abuse, instantly trapping numerous oppressors who had no idea of their guilt.

But perhaps the most successful strategy for manu-facturing grievances has been to highlight statistical differences between would-be victim groups and the general population. Any over- or under-representation of the group is taken as automatic proof of discrimination. In this book, Peter Saunders shows how fallacious and harmful this political strategy can be, and how far removed it is from our ideals of equality and justice.

Moral equality is the belief that every individual has the potential to judge right from wrong. From the view that we are moral equals, it has been inferred that people should not be treated differently solely because of inherited group characteristics such as race or gender. We each should be treated according to our personal qualities. But the culture of victimhood emphasises group identity rather than individual personality. The result has been a reversal of the liberal ideal that has been central to moral and political progress for hundreds of years, namely that we should judge each other according to the things we can change about ourselves, not the things we are stuck with.

As a first step towards the ideal of society based on moral equality and opportunity for all, we should abolish the Quango that has dedicated itself to inventing and legitimising victimhood and fanning the flames of grievance whenever the opportunity arises—the Equality and Human Rights Commission.

David G. Green
Director, Civitas

'Equality,' I spoke their word
As if a wedding vow,
Ah, but I was so much older then,
I'm younger than that now

Bob Dylan, *My Back Page*

1

What Kind of Equality?

On the far-flung islands of the Outer Hebrides, where many inhabitants still speak Scottish Gaelic and the Presbyterian Free Church of Scotland commands strong support, council leisure centres are closed on Sundays. Unlike most of the rest of the country, where Sunday has become just another day for shopping at the supermarket or going to the football, the inhabitants of the islands of Lewis, Harris and North Uist continue to observe the Sabbath, as their Bible and centuries of tradition require them to do. But now, the Equality and Human Rights Commission (EHRC) has advised the Western Isles council that it should open its leisure centres on Sundays.[1]

The EHRC was set up in 2006 to monitor the implementation of UK equalities legislation. Under this legislation, twenty-seven thousand government departments and public sector agencies now have a duty to promote equality between men and women, whites and blacks, heterosexuals, homosexuals, bisexuals and transsexuals, marrieds and singles, pregnant women and women who aren't pregnant, young and old people, those with disabilities and those without, and people of different faiths or none. The Western Isles council is one of the authorities covered by this legislation.

It is the need to ensure equality between people with different religious and philosophical beliefs that is causing the problem for the council, for it means it has a statutory duty to promote equality between its Christian inhabitants and atheists. According to the EHRC, this can only be achieved by opening its leisure centres on Sundays.

Why 'equality' requires that the Christians give in to the atheists on this issue is not entirely clear. The EHRC evidently believes that a locked community centre door on a Sunday represents 'discrimination' against non-believers, while an open one represents a 'neutral' and even-handed solution. But Sunday opening violates an article of faith for the church-going majority and will fundamentally shift community life in a direction in which they have no desire to go. The truth is that, like many of the issues to which equalities law is nowadays brought to bear, the question of whether the Western Isles community centres should continue to close on the Sabbath represents a zero-sum problem: if the atheists win, the Christians must lose, and vice versa. Whether it intends it or not, the EHRC is siding with the atheist minority.

How did we end up in a situation where unelected bureaucrats in London are allowed to micro-manage our lives in this way? In this short book, I look at how equalities legislation has developed during my adult lifetime from a set of simple rules designed to deter explicit racism, into a comprehensive, self-aggrandising, costly and intrusive surveillance industry interfering in the lives of millions of people. I show how compelling arguments in favour of protecting women and ethnic minorities from direct discrimination, which led to the early laws in the 1960s and 1970s, have been stretched and twisted in the years since to apply to all sorts of other groups who do not need, and should not require, such protection. I draw attention to the way 'discrimination' has been redefined so it is now possible to 'discriminate' against somebody without intending to, and how this has created a fear of committing unintentional thought crime which is squashing initiative and plain common sense out of the routine operations of all our public services. I expose the fallacy of equalities campaigners who assume that any evidence of group differences is a sign of discrimination, and I show how this is generating bad laws and misguided policies designed to remedy 'problems' that do not exist. Finally, I investigate the price we as a society are paying for all this monitoring, hectoring and special pleading.

Part of this price is financial. Employers lose thousands of pounds every time a disaffected employee, a disgruntled customer or an unsuccessful job applicant decides to haul them in front of a tribunal, and every large organisation now has to employ equalities and diversity officers to monitor its appointments and assess the impact of its operations on different sections of the population. All this costs millions of pounds every year, and customers and taxpayers end up footing the bill.

But we are also paying a heavy social price in terms of how we interact with each other. We have become a society where we are encouraged to embrace victimhood, where differences of achievement provoke knee-jerk charges of unfairness, where there is increasing resort to law whenever somebody loses out in a competition to someone else, and where individuals are disinclined to accept responsibility for what happens to them in their own lives, even when their own behaviour leads directly to their own misfortune. Underpinning all of this has been the growth of an enthusiastic and increasingly emboldened 'equalities industry' whose fundamental premise is that British society is 'unfair,' and that many of us are its victims.

3

Discrimination or difference?

It is not just the Western Isles Presbyterians who have got problems as a result of the equalities industry's activities. BBC Radio 4 is in trouble too.[2] In February 2011, the BBC Trust reported that too many Radio 4 listeners are white and middle class, and it urged the network to broaden its audience. Its research had revealed that only 28 per cent of Asian people and 41 per cent of black people are aware that Radio 4 exists, compared with 68 per cent of whites. The station is also more popular in the south than the north.

Because of the way modern managers and bureaucrats have been trained to regard statistics like these, the BBC Trust immediately knew when it saw these figures (a) that there was a 'problem' which needed sorting out, and (b) that the cause of the problem lay with the radio station itself. The Radio 4 audience is too middle class and too white, so Radio 4 has to change to become more 'inclusive'.

The Trust recommended that more ethnic minority people should be put on air, that more ethnic minority drama writers should be recruited, and that BBC managers should do more to promote the station among 'minority ethnic opinion formers'. To raise the station's listening figures among working-class northerners, it further recommended that programmes like *Gardeners' Question Time* and *The Food Programme* should be broadcast from high-profile northern events and venues.[3] All of this was necessary, not to improve the quality of the programmes, but to counter 'social exclusion' among potential black and working class listeners.

It appears not to have occurred to the Trust that different radio stations might be expected to appeal to different kinds of audiences, that there is nothing wrong with audience segmentation and specialisation (especially when literally thousands of different stations are now available via digital radio), and that a more diverse audience could only be achieved by diluting and ultimately destroying the distinctiveness that current Radio 4 listeners appreciate.[4] Evidence of different outcomes—that whites listen more than blacks, and that the middle classes appreciate the station in greater numbers than the working classes—is assumed to indicate the existence of some sort of 'social exclusion,' when really, all it demonstrates is that we want and appreciate different things.

Confused and muddled thinking like this is now widespread throughout the public services. Not just the BBC, but the police, the universities, the civil service and the hospitals all now panic when statisticians tell them that their user profiles differ from the social norm. If black youths get arrested in greater numbers than white youths, or if kids from public schools get into Oxbridge in greater numbers than those from state comprehensives, or if more Pakistani babies die in infancy than white babies, the immediate assumption is that the institutions—the police, the universities, the maternity hospitals—must have been operating unfairly. Whenever one social group stands out from another on some observed characteristic, it is assumed that 'discrimination' and 'inequality' are the cause, and that the organisation itself must be at fault. More monitoring and more reforms are then prescribed to root the problem out.

This lazy and pernicious way of thinking has come about as a direct result of the unchecked rise of the equalities industry over the last 40 or 50 years. This industry now employs thousands of people who spend their time looking for social differences, linking them to real or imagined 'unfair' practices, and then imposing 'solutions' involving the political re-education of offenders, imposition of quotas, rewriting of procedures and instigation of legal proceedings to rectify the 'harm' that has been done. These people operate like the witch-finders of the seventeenth century, swooping on communities which didn't even realise they had a problem, rooting out unsuspecting perpetrators, extracting confessions, and then purging the evil before moving on to their next target.

Like the witch-finders of old, the equality industry's claims rarely get challenged, for most prominent politicians, academics and social affairs commentators today are scared of saying anything lest they themselves get accused of bigotry and have the finger pointed at them.[5] The result is that the equalities industry goes from strength to strength, its tentacles spreading into almost every nook and cranny of daily life. It is time we did some pruning.

The three aspects of equality

Everybody is in favour of equality. It is inscribed on the two great banners which ushered in our modern age: in the slogan of the French Revolution ('Liberty, Equality, Fraternity'), and in the resounding rhetoric of the American Declaration of Independence ('All men are created equal'). How, living in the twenty-first century shadow of these two epoch-forming events, could we not support equality? How, indeed, could we respond other than gratefully to those who work diligently and tirelessly to defend and extend it?

But it all depends on what kind of equality we are talking about. The word has at least three, distinct applications.

First, there is *formal equality*, or the equality associated with common citizenship rights. According to T.H. Marshall, who wrote a celebrated essay back in 1950 charting the historical development of citizenship rights in England,[6] formal equality consists of three elements which have evolved over several centuries:

- *Legal equality* is the principle that everybody should be subject to the same rules and laws. From the king downwards, we are all required to obey the same laws, applied on the same criteria by the same courts, and penalties for wrong-doers are the same, irrespective of their birth or social standing. Marshall says this principle of legal equality was established in England by the eighteenth century.

- *Political equality* is the principle that every adult should be able to participate fully in the democratic procedures of government. We all have a vote of equal value, and we are all free to put ourselves up for election. We also enjoy the crucial political freedoms of free speech, free assembly and a free press. According to Marshall, this principle of political equality became established in England in the nineteenth century, although women did not achieve full political equality until the 1920s.

- *Social equality* is the principle that everyone should have a right to a minimum level of material support necessary to maintain themselves and their families. Marshall saw the establishment of the welfare state in the twentieth century as establishing this third, key component of modern citizenship, and whatever we may think about the way the welfare state has grown since he was writing, the key point is that everyone has an equal right to make a claim for support, based

7

on a common set of rules of eligibility and entitlement.

Although there may be disputes at the margins — should people suspected of terrorist offences be detained without trial?; should prisoners be allowed to vote?; should recent immigrants be entitled to claim full welfare services? — these three elements of formal equality are widely accepted today, and nobody seriously challenges them in principle. If we were to discover that one group in the population was being denied due process, or was being stripped of voting rights, or was being excluded from welfare services, simply because of its race, religion or gender, most of us would be outraged, and rightly so. When the French and American revolutionaries rose up in the name of equality, it was this kind of formal equality they were talking about, and the principle is now firmly embedded in all western cultures.

A second aspect of equality is *equality of opportunity*. This is much more problematic — not because there is any major disagreement about its desirability, but because there are some obvious, major obstacles in the way of its fulfilment.

The principle of equality of opportunity holds that every individual should be in a position to achieve the best they can in life, given their talent and a willingness to work hard. This is the bedrock idea behind the ideal of a 'meritocracy,' to which many of us subscribe.[7] In general, we approve of the idea of an open society where bright and hard-working people can rise to the top positions regardless of their origins, and we disapprove of people using privileges of birth to secure advantages for themselves or their children to which others cannot gain access. We want the competition for prizes to be fair, and this means everyone must line up together at the starting point.

The fundamental requirement if this is to be achieved is equal access to education. In the UK, we have arguably had this condition in place for many decades (certainly ever since the 1944 Education Act), and with the recent, remarkable, expansion of higher education, there is no reason in principle why young people of ability should not attain all the training and qualifications they need to exploit their talents to the full, irrespective of their social background.[8]

Elsewhere I have reviewed the evidence on social mobility, down as well as up the occupational class system, and have shown that Britain is a remarkably open society which recruits people to positions of higher pay, status and authority largely on the basis of their ability and effort.[9] But we are not a *perfect* meritocracy. Social class origins do still play a part in shaping people's destinies, albeit a relatively small part. It helps if your parents have contacts in the City, if they send you to a good public school, or if they are sufficiently interested in your development to attend parents' evenings and to instil in you high aspirations and a sense of self-efficacy. It's not simply, or even mainly, a question of money; the key thing seems to be quality parenting, and not all children get it.[10]

This is why it is so difficult to deliver genuine equality of opportunity, even though we might all believe in it as a principle. Initiatives like the Blair Government's Sure Start programme and the Coalition Government's pupil premium are worthwhile attempts to compensate for the bad parenting and poor schooling that some children experience. But there is only so much a government can do to enable bright children to succeed. Short of rounding up all infants at birth and corralling them in state nurseries to ensure they all get exactly the same start in life, we have to accept that what sociologists call 'cultural capital' is unequally endowed between families, and some children will always enjoy advantages over others simply by virtue of having been born to more caring and supportive parents.

The third aspect of equality is *equality of outcomes*. This is where everyone ends up with roughly the same wealth and status irrespective of their work or talents,[11] and it has been the dream of egalitarians down the ages. In its most radical version, 'pure communism', people contribute what they can to the collective coffers and take out only what they need. According to Karl Marx, this is how human beings used to live when we were simple hunters and gatherers, but once we learned how to grow crops and domesticate animals, people started establishing private property claims, and some piled up resources while others became enslaved. Marx held out the prospect of a return to this communist idyll at some far-off point in the future, when he believed modern technology would be able to produce as much as any of us want or need. But even he recognised that until human beings can be re-socialised out of their acquisitive instincts, the best we can hope for is a socialist system of distribution where people are rewarded according to the value of the work they perform.[12]

Modern-day egalitarians tend to go further than Marx's socialist prescription, for they not only want to reduce or abolish so-called 'unearned incomes' (e.g. rents from land, profits from shares), but they also want earned incomes from work compressed by higher taxes on higher earners, and benefits paid to people who do not work to be made more generous. These arguments have traditionally been made on ethical grounds, but recently, left intellectuals have begun to argue that radical tax and welfare policies are also a matter of practical necessity if modern societies are to function harmoniously. They claim that we would all benefit from increased equality of outcomes, for even the richest people would end up leading happier lives in a more equal society where people are more contented and less competitive.[13]

The evidence used to support this assertion is shaky, and the analysis is full of holes, but arguments like this have nevertheless been attracting widespread support among egalitarian idealists in the last couple of years.[14] Complete equality of outcomes can never be secured, of course, but many intellectuals and political activists still aspire to a much more compressed distribution of income and wealth than we currently have, and many of them think there is a compelling case for it.

You can't please all the people all the time

One obvious problem which all egalitarians face is that the three aspects of equality which we have outlined here, all of which they profess to support, are incompatible. It was Friedrich Hayek who pointed out that formal equality is bound to generate inequalities of outcomes for as long as individuals are endowed with different capacities and are motivated to pursue different objectives: 'From the fact that people are very different it follows that, if we treat them equally, the result must be inequality in their actual position, and that the only way to place them in an equal position would be to treat them differently. Equality before the law and material equality are therefore not only different but are in conflict with each other.'[15] Apply the same rule to people with different qualities and you will end up with unequal results.

11

It is precisely because of this dilemma that many people feel uneasy about affirmative action and positive discrimination programmes which are designed to increase equality of opportunity by giving people from the least favoured groups an initial leg up. Policies like these only work by destroying formal equality, for different applicants for a job or a university place are assessed on different criteria according to their sex, or which ethnic group they come from.

Similarly, many people feel queasy about income redistribution schemes intended to bring about greater equality of outcomes, for redistribution not only undermines formal equality (people get treated differently according to their circumstances), but it nullifies the rationale for equality of opportunity (those who have been successful are penalised). Where is the point in making people equal at the start of a race if we then hobble the leaders half way through to ensure that they all cross the finishing line together?

Believing in equality is therefore a much more complicated matter than might initially be assumed. Recognising this, any wise government might be well advised to exercise extreme caution before publishing an ambitious 'Equality Strategy', for this is bound to be a path strewn with unforeseen obstacles and pitfalls.

Equal treatment + equal opportunity = equal outcomes?

In December 2010, the new Coalition Government published its 'Equality Strategy'. The document insisted that inequality in Britain is a serious problem which requires further change in people's attitudes and behaviour.[16] As evidence for this, it pointed out that men, on average, earn more than women; blacks have higher unemployment rates than whites; middle-class people tend to live longer than working-class people; gypsy children achieve fewer GCSE passes than white children, and black Caribbean children get excluded from school more than children from other ethnic backgrounds. It thought that all these differences pointed to our 'failure to tackle discrimination'.[17]

The Minister for Women and Equalities, Theresa May, assures us in the Preface to this document that: 'Equality is at the heart of this Coalition Government. It is fundamental to building a strong economy and a fair society... Equality is key to all our work.'[18] But what exactly does she mean by equality?

The document says the government wants to pursue the first two of aspects of equality identified above — formal equality and equality of opportunity: 'Equality can mean many different things to many different people. This strategy focuses on two principles of equality: equal treatment and equal opportunity.'[19] Nothing is said explicitly about the third aspect, equality of outcomes. But it is evidence about unequal outcomes — male and female pay rates, black and white unemployment rates, middle-class and working-class death rates, and so on — that provides the rationale for having an equality strategy in the first place. This concern with unequal outcomes turns out to be the hidden, third element on which the entire strategy is founded.

Consider, for example, the battle which the government has picked with some of our top universities over entry requirements. The principle of formal equality requires simply that all candidates be assessed on the same criteria, and this, by and large, is what universities have been doing for many years. If you want to go to Oxford or Cambridge, you need to get top A-level grades no matter who you are, and you won't get a place without them.

But soon after coming to power, Deputy Prime Minister Nick Clegg and Higher Education minister David Willetts began attacking Britain's top universities for admitting too few state school children from poor backgrounds.[20] The claim was that Oxbridge was somehow 'excluding' less privileged applicants while giving an inside track to those from top schools with rich parents. So convinced did the government become that there was a problem that when it gave universities the right to charge higher fees, it linked it with a new duty to submit plans showing how they intended to admit more lower-class applicants in the future. Essentially, the universities were being told to take more lower-class applicants on lower grades.

In April 2011, the debate widened from social class to race when Prime Minister Cameron made a speech attacking Oxford University as 'disgraceful' because it admitted so few black students. Oxford countered with statistics showing that, in addition to its 12,671 white students in 2009-10, it had 1,477 Asian students, 1,098 Chinese, 838 mixed-race, 254 'other ethnicity' and 253 describing themselves as 'black'. A University spokesman angrily pointed out that almost a quarter of its students were from ethnic minority backgrounds, and he emphasised that Oxford was 'fully committed to admitting the most able students regardless of background'. He also noted that across the whole country in 2009-10, only 432 black students achieved the minimum A-level scores required for Oxbridge entry.[21]

This battle over higher education entry criteria demonstrates two crucial lessons. First, it shows how attempts to increase equality of opportunity inevitably end up chipping away at formal equality (even though the government says it wants to promote both). In this case, promoting opportunities for lower class and black students to go to Oxbridge in greater numbers led straight away to the demand that entry requirements be changed for candidates from these backgrounds.[22] If the universities buckle under this pressure, it will mean one set of eligibility rules for rich kids, and another for poor ones. If your parents educate you in the private sector, you will have to be 'more equal' than your competitors from comprehensive schools if you are to secure a place ahead of them.

Secondly, this unhappy story also shows how unequal outcomes unthinkingly get used as evidence of unequal treatment (even though the government says it is not interested in promoting equality of outcomes). It is because Oxbridge admits fewer state school entrants, relative to their numbers in the whole population, that ministers have convinced themselves that the admissions procedures must be at fault. Similarly, it is because there are relatively few black Caribbean students at Oxford that Mr Cameron thinks the University must be treating ethnic minority candidates unfairly. Because the *outcomes* have been found to be unequal, the assumption is automatically made that the *procedures* must be unfair.

Despite what it says in its Equality Strategy, therefore, it turns out that the Coalition government is committed to the most radical form of egalitarian thinking—the belief in equal outcomes. Its strategy starts out from the unspoken assumption that we would all turn out the same if only the procedures were fair and the opportunities were widely available. When it then finds that we don't all turn out the same—that more public school pupils get to Cambridge, or that fewer black

Caribbean pupils get to Oxford—it is enough to convince the government of the existence somewhere in the system of unfairness and discrimination, and of the need to intervene to 'do something' to rectify it.

We have encountered this same logic before, in the BBC Trust's complaints about Radio 4. Just as the Trust believes there must be a problem of racial exclusion at the BBC because fewer black people than white listen to Radio 4, so too government ministers think there must be a problem of racial exclusion in the university sector because fewer black people than white go to Oxford. In neither case is any attempt made to offer evidence of discriminatory actions or procedures in operation. It is enough simply to note that the outcomes differ.

Arguing from evidence on differential outcomes to impute the existence of unfair causes is, of course, illogical and fallacious, for it fails to appreciate that unequal outcomes may be the result of 'fair' procedures. Most people would think it perfectly fair, for example, that children who work hard at school should end up with better exam results than their less motivated classmates. We shall see in chapter 9 that this is almost certainly the explanation for why children from some ethnic backgrounds (notably Indian and Chinese) do so much better in our schools than those from others (including whites and black Caribbean).

But the problem is not just that so much of current equalities policy is illogical. It is also that these policies can be positively dangerous, for forcing equal outcomes onto people with different characteristics and attributes can produce very 'unfair' results. If we insisted that Oxbridge turn away Chinese and Indian applicants because they are 'over-represented' among those scoring top A-level grades, for example, we would create the more equal outcomes that the government wants, but at the cost of a grossly unfair selection process.

Unfortunately, however, this twisted, Procrustean logic now pervades all UK public policy making. It infects the Tory Party, the BBC and many other august bodies besides. The template has been set by the Equality and Human Rights Commission—the body which is insisting that the people of the Western Isles open their leisure centres on Sundays.

In 2010, the EHRC published a 750-page report entitled *How Fair is Britain*? In his Foreword to the report, the Commission's chair, Trevor Phillips, assured us: 'We are not as yet a fair society.' He justified this conclusion by referring to all the evidence gathered in the report that different sections of the British population vary in the jobs they do, the exams they pass, the diseases they catch and the prison sentences they serve. For Phillips, such evidence of group variation demonstrates the existence of 'an invisible, many-stranded web of prejudice, inertia and unfairness that holds so many back'.[23]

But the EHRC, the BBC Trust and the Prime Minister are all guilty of the same error. The test of fairness does not lie in outcomes. It lies in processes. We shall see in the chapters that follow that there is precious little evidence that the 'web of prejudice and inertia' imagined by Phillips even exists, still less that it has a significant causal impact on our lives.

2

Too Much of a Good Thing?

Outlawing racial discrimination

When I was growing up in England in the 1950s and early 1960s, employers could, if they wished, advertise job vacancies as available only to white applicants. People with rooms to let in their houses used to place cards in their front bay windows saying 'No Coloureds', and estate agents sometimes refused to show black families houses they had for sale on all-white estates. Shops, pubs and restaurants could, if they were so minded, refuse to serve black customers. Discrimination on grounds of race was not illegal in post-war Britain, and it was not uncommon either.[1]

Racial discrimination gradually came to be officially recognised as a problem after substantial numbers of immigrants began to arrive in Britain from the early 1950s. Britain had long been home to a wide diversity of national and ethnic minority groups, but most people coming to live here from overseas had assimilated into the local culture without much difficulty. In 1948, however, Parliament passed the British Nationality Act which gave 800 million people living throughout the former Empire the right to come to Britain to live and work, and this triggered a significant increase in non-white immigration, which led to rising tensions with the host population in many of the areas where they settled.

Immigration from the so-called 'New Commonwealth' (mainly the Caribbean and the Indian subcontinent) rose from just 3,000 per year in the early 1950s to 136,400 in

18

1961. Britain's non-white population rose to half-a-million in less than ten years. Alarmed by the rising levels of hostility this provoked among some sections of the native, white population, Parliament passed a series of Immigration Acts from 1962 onwards designed to limit the flow. But despite these new controls, two-and-a-half million more immigrants arrived from the 'New Commonwealth' after 1962. Their total numbers today are around four million.[2]

As the number of black and Asian immigrants coming to Britain rose, so racial hostility and tensions escalated, particularly in and around the areas where they settled in large concentrations. Sometimes, as in Notting Hill in 1958, these tensions exploded into violence, but more commonly, they simmered in an atmosphere of suspicion and mutual fear. In a study of Caribbean immigrants in South London in the mid-1950s, Sheila Patterson found that many white workers regarded black newcomers as a threat to their jobs, and white employers often responded to these fears by imposing informal quotas on the number of 'coloured' workers they employed.[3] Nor was racial exclusion limited to employment. In Birmingham, three-quarters of people polled in 1956 thought some kind of 'colour bar' was operating in the city's bars and restaurants,[4] and a study by John Rex and Robert Moore showed how newly-arrived immigrants to the city were being excluded from both local authority and owner-occupied housing estates by the operation of tacit (and sometimes explicit) racial selection procedures.[5]

Two Acts of Parliament eventually challenged racist practices like these. In 1965, the Race Relations Act made it a civil tort for businesses such as hotels, pubs, restaurants, theatres, cinemas, swimming baths and public transport operators to discriminate in the provision of their services on the basis of someone's race or colour. Individuals who believed they had been the victim of repeated discrimination could refer their case to a local conciliation committee, which would seek redress on their behalf. If the issue could not be resolved, it would then be referred to a new Race Relations Board to investigate, and it could in turn refer the matter to the Attorney General to institute civil proceedings and, if necessary, to seek an injunction.[6] All of this was very new (there was no equivalent body to the Race Relations Board in British administrative law at that time), and it was very, very tentative. Parliament was feeling its way in unfamiliar territory.

The idea of using criminal sanctions to deter discriminatory behaviour was considered but eventually rejected because higher standards of proof would be required than for civil offences. There was also a concern that juries might be reluctant to convict in criminal cases. The 1965 Act did, however, create a new criminal offence of 'incitement to racial hatred'. The 1936 Public Order Act had already made speeches illegal if they were likely to cause a breach of the peace (i.e. hostile action), but this new legislation specifically outlawed speeches or the distribution of leaflets in a public place which had the intention of stirring up racial hatred (i.e. hostile thoughts). Parliament said this new law should only be invoked in 'an extreme and very bad case', and even then, only against the 'ringleaders' of racial incitement.[7]

The 1965 legislation was followed in 1968 by a second, and much stronger, Race Relations Act which extended the scope of the public services covered by anti-discrimination law to include education and financial services. It also made it unlawful to discriminate 'on the ground of colour, race or ethnic or national origins' in the two key areas of employment and housing, and it became illegal to publish a discriminatory advertisement or notice pertaining to any area of activity (not just those explicitly covered by the Act).[8] The Race Relations Board was given the power to bring cases to court itself, rather than referring them to the Attorney General, and it was no longer necessary to prove repeated discrimination—one instance was enough to trigger an investigation.

By 1968, freedom from racial discrimination had effectively been recognised by Parliament as a new legal right.

Rights are claims on other people

All rights involve legally-enforceable claims on other people, so one person's new right is necessarily another's restriction on liberty. By giving individuals the right to claim access to services, jobs or housing regardless of their race or nationality, Parliament was limiting the right of service providers, employers and property owners to choose their clients, employees or tenants as they saw fit. In this sense, the 1965 and 1968 Acts shifted the balance between 'civil rights' and 'property rights' in Britain in favour of the former.

If you offered rooms to let in your house, for example, it was now illegal to refuse to let a room to a black tenant, even though it was your property. If you had your own small business, it was illegal if you decided only to employ white workers, even though you were paying the wages. And, as far-right activist Robert Relf demonstrated in 1976, when he put up a sign outside his house in Leamington Spa offering it for sale 'to an English family only', if you were advertising something for sale, you were not allowed to limit the range of races or nationalities to whom you were willing to sell it, even though the goods in question were yours to dispose of. In all these cases, the law now specified that the right to receive non-discriminatory treatment from others overrode the traditional right to decide how to use or dispose of your own property.

Few people today would consider this limitation on the rights of property owners and businesses to be unjustified or excessive. Looking back, it seems extra-ordinary that boarding houses were ever allowed to turn away tenants because of their race, or that pubs could refuse to serve black customers. Such distressing examples of racial hostility and exclusion offend most people's sense of fairness, and it is doubtful whether many of us would want to turn the legislative clock back.

Yet once Parliament challenged the principle that people have the right to be selective in the beneficial use of their own property, we crossed an important line. From now on, the right to demand that employers and service providers should behave in specific ways could and would be pushed into an ever-wider range of areas as diverse 'victim groups' sought to harness the power of the State to impose their ever-increasing range of demands. Why limit the law to the regulation of public services, employment and housing, for example? Why limit it to relations between ethnic and racial groups? And why limit it to overt examples of discriminatory behaviour? In 1965, Parliament opened a Pandora's Box, and we have been dealing with the consequences ever since.

Getting the balance right

Over the last 50 years, equalities laws have been extended to cover an increasing range of activities, and to encompass increasing numbers of victims. The days when a boarding house proprietor might put a notice in the window saying 'No Coloureds' are far behind us; in today's Britain, B&B proprietors who insist that couples must be married if they want to share a room can successfully be sued.[9]

From modest beginnings in the sixties, equalities laws have multiplied to a point where it is now legitimate to ask if we have gone too far, or have got the balance wrong. The right of individuals to be protected against discrimination has been strengthened, but the right to behave and think in ways the government or others in authority might disapprove of has been undermined as a result. This raises the obvious danger that some people's preferences are being unfairly privileged in law relative to others.

We saw one example of this at the start of this book, where we noted how Christians in the Outer Hebrides are being forced by equalities laws to abandon their Sunday observance rules so that atheists might organise dances and other events in community halls. But this is just one, small illustration of how these laws get used to benefit one section of the population to the detriment of others.

Consider, for example, the laws which prohibit employers from discriminating among job applicants on grounds of age or disability. These laws mean that candidates are protected from discrimination, but they are not the only people with a legitimate interest in the outcome of appointments. When a school appoints a new teacher, for example, parents have a legitimate interest in the outcome. They might want their children taught by a young teacher (about half the population thinks people over 70 make unsuitable primary school teachers), but equalities laws prevent schools from making appoint-ments designed to achieve a particular age balance on their staff. Parents (and head teachers) are also unlikely to want to appoint someone who will need to take a lot of time off through illness, or who suffer debilitating depressions, but again, they are not allowed to appoint (or dismiss) teachers on these grounds.[10] The question is: why should the law privilege the interests of potential candidates over those of their future employers or clients?

Similar questions can be raised about other dimensions of equality law, such as the right of gay couples to adopt children. This affirmation of homosexual equality with heterosexuals has been an important objective of gay rights activists, but it has had serious, negative consequences for other parties. Some Roman Catholic adoption agencies have had to close, because this ruling forces them to follow procedures which violate their Christian ethics. More importantly, perhaps, there is also the awkward question of whether children have a legitimate right to be given both a mother and a father when authorities place them in an 'appropriate' home. Why should the right of gay men to adopt a child outweigh the right of a child to have a mum?

In both of these examples, as in the Outer Hebrides case, the law recognises the right of individuals not to be discriminated against. But what happens when this right runs up against the legitimate preferences and expectations of other parties who might want to discriminate for perfectly reasonable and understandable reasons?

Running with or against the grain

Any application of rules and laws results in winners and losers. These outcomes generally get accepted in liberal, democratic societies because most people recognise the laws as just. Traditionally, laws give expression to social norms which are widely held and deeply respected throughout society. We prohibit theft, assault, fraud and so on because almost everybody feels such behaviours are morally wrong, and those who engage in them pose a threat to the stability and happiness of the entire community.

This consensus is, however, much less in evidence in our current equalities laws, where there is widespread disagreement about some of the issues the law is trying to regulate.

Surveys suggest, for example, that half the population believes B&B proprietors should be allowed to decline bookings by gay couples who wish to share a room in their house, and about a quarter think they should be able to turn away youngsters. More than half the population disagrees with giving extra help to disabled candidates applying for jobs. And while a quarter of the population thinks the government should give more protection for people with strong religious beliefs, another quarter thinks it is already doing too much in this area.[11]

This jumble of assorted opinions reflects the fact that equalities legislation has generally been imposed from above, rather than (or as well as) giving expression to new values evolving from below. For almost fifty years, progressive politicians have been introducing laws designed to *change* the way people think and behave about issues like these, rather than to *reflect* them. Especially in more recent times, the law has been used as an ideological battering ram, both by Westminster politicians and by Brussels, to forcibly redefine social norms. This use of state power to change public opinion and behaviour is not necessarily 'wrong' (I argue in chapter 3 that the introduction of race and sex discrimination laws between 1965 and 1975 was justifiable, for example), but it does help explain why such legislation has often failed to achieve legitimacy in the eyes of many ordinary people.

Newspaper editors know this, which is why they regularly run stories of 'political correctness gone mad'. They know these stories will resonate with many of their readers who sense that the law is grating against their intuitive sense of natural justice, rather than reflecting it. Most people feel helpless to do anything about this. They just smile and shrug their shoulders in mute recognition of the way the law has become increasingly disconnected from the everyday mores of the community it serves. But every time this happens, respect for the law and the legislative process erodes a little further.

In the next three chapters we shall see that UK equalities legislation has been over-extended in three important ways:

- The law has been extended to sections of the population which should not need statutory protection (chapter 3).

- Laws have penalised 'discrimination' even where there is no intention to discriminate (chapter 4).

- Legislation has given special privileges and protections to favoured sections of the population, breaking the principle that everybody should have the same rights, and shifting power from Parliament to the judiciary (chapter 5).

All three of these developments have undermined the principle of formal, or blind, justice and have weakened the legitimacy of the law itself in the eyes of many ordinary British people.

3

Too Many Victims

Beyond race and sex

In the sixties, even as the new race discrimination laws were being fashioned and debated, reformist MPs were also trying to introduce private members' bills seeking to extend protection to other groups in the population such as women, older people and those with disabilities. It was only a matter of time before Parliament would legislate to extend anti-discrimination protection to these other groups, and the first to benefit were women.

In 1970, it was made illegal under the Equal Pay Act for employers to pay male and female employees different rates, or to give them different conditions of employment, if they were doing the same job, or different jobs of equal value.[1] Companies were given five years to adjust their pay rates to this new requirement. Once the Act was implemented in December 1975, any employee who believed they were being underpaid because of their sex could take their employer to an industrial (later, employment) tribunal.[2] If their claim was successful, an equality clause could be inserted into their contract of employment and arrears could be awarded covering up to six years of previous employment.

An obvious danger created by the Equal Pay Act was that some firms might replace their (hitherto cheaper) female staff with men, or would further segregate men's and women's work to make comparison of their pay rates difficult or impossible to achieve.[3] To combat these possibilities, the 1975 Sex Discrimination Act made it unlawful to recruit, dismiss, train, promote or transfer employees on the basis of their sex (later judgements extended this to include their marital status or pregnancy), unless there were genuine requirements of the occupation which made such selection necessary (e.g. recruiting a male actor for a male role in a play). The Act also had the effect of outlawing harassment and victimisation of employees who brought sex discrimination cases, or who gave evidence in such cases, and it established a new Equal Opportunities Commission to promote equality between men and women and to monitor the operation of the sex equality laws.

The Equal Opportunities Commission became the second statutory body (after the Race Relations Board, which became the Commission for Racial Equality in 1976) with powers to monitor and enforce equality rules. It consisted of a chair, deputy chair and thirteen part-time members, and they were supported by more than 100 staff based in Manchester (Wales and Scotland were run from sub-offices, and Northern Ireland had its own, equivalent body). They spent their time advising individuals who were taking employers to tribunals under the equal pay and sex discrimination laws, issuing codes of practice to employers, and launching their own investigations of suspected malpractice. A new 'equalities industry' was beginning to emerge.

Both pieces of sex equality legislation came into force at the same time, at the end of 1975.[4] Since then, women have also won the right to retire at the same age as men (under 1986 legislation), and transsexuals have won the right to change their officially-recognised sexual identity (following a ruling from the European Court of Human Rights, the 2004 Gender Recognition Act gave transsexuals the right to obtain a new birth certificate, and to be treated under law according to their new identity).[5]

After race and sex came disability. The 1995 Disability Discrimination Act (which was further amended in 2005) defined 'disability' as 'a physical or mental impairment which has a substantial and long-term adverse effect on [a person's] ability to carry out normal day-to-day activities'.[6] Unlike the race and sex laws that preceded it, protection was now being extended to people on the basis of what they could and could not *do*, rather than what they *are* (although ironically, many people covered by the legislation do not think of themselves as disabled).[7] It made it unlawful to discriminate against somebody with a disability in the areas of employment, provision of goods and services, land and property deals and education, and it issued regulations setting out access standards for public transport. Discrimination was allowed, however, where it could be justified by the nature of the job (e.g. the armed forces were still allowed to turn down recruits on grounds of ill health). Employment discrimination cases could be taken to a tribunal; other cases were to be heard in county court.[8]

As we shall see later, this legislation also broke new ground by placing a *positive duty* on employers and service providers to make 'reasonable adjustments' to allow disabled people to overcome obstacles that lead to them being treated differently from other people. Employers might, for example, be expected to provide disabled employees with helpers, shops might have to add wheelchair ramps for their customers, and businesses might be required to issue leaflets in large type for clients whose sight is impaired. Small businesses with fewer than 15 employees were exempted from these requirements, but for everybody else, failure to make such adjustments could now constitute unlawful discrimination.

For the first time, the law was requiring employers and service providers to take actions to prevent an unequal outcome from occurring. It had moved beyond simply limiting the rights of property owners to use their assets as they choose; now it was telling them what they must do. A Disability Rights Commission was established with similar responsibilities and powers to the Equal Opportunities Commission, but also with the additional task of advising employers and others on the kinds of adjustments they could be required to undertake. So now there were three equalities commissions.

Equality law was further extended in 2003 when EU employment directives prohibiting discrimination on grounds of sexual orientation and religion and belief were enacted. This marked another major step, for the law was now protecting certain kinds of *behaviours and beliefs*, whereas before it had been limited to protecting people with certain defined *attributes* or *capabilities*. These new statutory instruments were phrased in almost exactly the same way as earlier UK equalities legislation affecting other victim groups, and like these earlier laws, they also made it an offence to harass or victimise anybody seeking redress under these provisions.[9]

Three years after that, again reflecting an EU employment directive, a further statutory instrument was laid before Parliament making it unlawful for employers to discriminate on grounds of age when appointing, promoting or training people.[10] This also made it illegal for an employer forcibly to retire any member of staff under the age of 65, and in 2011, much to the consternation of employer organisations, the government announced that it was scrapping the default retirement age altogether. This means employees will now be able to continue in work indefinitely, and if employers want to get rid of them, they will have to justify their dismissal in the same way as they would any younger workers.[11] Employees found to have been victims of unlawful age discrimination may be awarded unlimited damages.[12]

Also in 2006, a new Equality Act extended the existing employment protection enjoyed by religious believers and gays, lesbians and bisexuals to include discrimination in the provision of goods and services, education, public functions and property. The Act also strengthened existing sex equality law by creating a new duty on public authorities to *promote* equality between men and women (the so-called 'gender duty' — a similar duty to promote racial equality had been introduced a few years earlier). This meant that the positive obligation to prevent unequal outcomes, which had first been introduced in respect of disabled people, had now been extended to relations between the sexes and between different ethnic groups as well.[13]

The 2006 Act also established a new Equality and Human Rights Commission (EHRC) to take over the work and duties of the three existing commissions for racial equality, equal opportunities (gender) and disability.[14]

Bringing it all together

Recognising how cluttered the equalities legislation was becoming, the Labour government in 2010 passed a new Equality Act which replaced all the existing laws, consolidating and in some cases extending them in a single piece of legislation. The new Act identified nine 'protected characteristics' to be covered by anti-discrimination law: age, disability, gender reassignment (transsexuals, transvestites and transgendered people), marriage or civil partnership, pregnancy and maternity, race, religion or belief (including 'any philosophical belief'), sex, and sexual orientation (gay, lesbian or bisexual). It then spelled out seven different ways in which behaviour might be deemed 'discriminatory' in relation to any of these nine characteristics.

'*Direct discrimination*' (treating somebody less favourably than somebody else) is ruled out for all nine of the protected groups, although the Act made an exception of disability where it explicitly permitted disabled people to be treated *more* favourably than other people.[15] Under this new law, it is unlawful for a prospective employer to ask a candidate about their health, or their record of absences at previous jobs, and taking action against an employee for taking too many sick days can be deemed unlawful if these absences are a direct result of their disability.[16]

Secondly, the Act outlawed '*indirect discrimination,*' which is where a common set of rules or procedures puts a protected group at a disadvantage relative to other people (this is explained more fully in chapter 4). This notion of indirect discrimination was built into almost all the legislation from 1975 onwards, so the 2010 Act merely reaffirmed it for all the protected groups.

The other five types of unlawful discrimination identified by the Act were: '*associative discrimination,*' where someone is unfairly treated because of their association with someone else with a protected characteristic (e.g. discrimination against somebody caring for a disabled person); '*harassment,*' which is behaviour deemed offensive by somebody belonging to a protected group; '*third party harassment*' (if, for example, a customer tells a racist joke to which another customer objects, the owner of the business could be guilty of third party harassment); *'victimisation'* of anybody who brings a case under the equalities law; and *'discrimination by perception'* (direct discrimination against somebody whom others believe to be in a protected group, even though they are not—e.g. sacking a woman who is believed to be pregnant, even though she isn't).

The Act also extended the 'public sector duty' under which all public organisations, including government departments, local authorities, the courts, police and prison service, NHS Trusts, school governors, colleges and universities, and the BBC must report every year on the progress they are making towards achieving equality. They were already required to report on race, disability and gender equality as a result of the duty established under the 2006 Act, but the 2010 Act added age, sexual orientation, religion or belief, pregnancy and maternity, and gender reassignment to this list.[17] This means all public sector bodies may now be required to assemble and publish data on how all the different protected groups perform on relevant measures (e.g. things like exam results for schools; survival rates for hospitals; or stop and search statistics for police forces). They must also provide details of their own staffing profiles (e.g. the proportion of staff from ethnic minorities, the 'gender pay gap' between average male and female earnings in the organisation, their record in recruiting disabled people into senior positions, and so on).[18] All of this is in addition to their existing responsibilities to carry out Equality Impact Assessments on any new policies they introduce.

Part I of the 2010 Equality Act also created a new public sector duty to reduce inequalities deriving from 'socio-economic disadvantage'. This effectively meant that social class was now being added to the list of protected characteristics, and public bodies would have to start recruiting more people who had been born into lower-class households. However, the new Coalition Government announced shortly after it came into office that it would not implement this part of the legislation.[19]

The Government Equalities Office insisted when the 2010 Act was passed that it would reduce bureaucracy. It is hard to know whether to credit such a statement to Orwell or Kafka.

Who should be protected?

David Green has added up the number of women, disabled people, elderly people, ethnic minorities, non-Christian people of faith, and gays in Britain, and comes to the conclusion that about three-quarters of the population now belongs to at least one 'protected' potential victim group. If we allow for 'multiple discrimination' (and the 2010 Act explicitly allows people to bring cases if they think they are being discriminated against because of a combination of two characteristics), we reach a figure of 109 per cent of the population.[20]

Did we need to go this far? If there was a good argument for protecting ethnic minorities and women against discrimination back in the 1960s and 1970s, does this necessarily mean there was an equally compelling case for extending this protection later on to disabled people, the elderly, gays and lesbians, transsexuals, religious minorities, and all the other assorted categories which achieved recognition in the 2010 Act?

It is no accident that discrimination on the basis of *race* and *sex* were the first two categories to be legislated, for these are what sociologists call our 'basic' social roles.[21] Your sex and race are, in most cases, ascribed at birth, and are very hard (for most people, impossible) to change in the course of your life. Because of this, they strongly influence the way people think of themselves—their identity—and they bear on many different aspects of their lives. They are crucial aspects of 'who we are', yet they are things we can do very little to change.

It is for this reason that most people consider it unfair and unethical to discriminate against people because they are, for example, black or female. Your race and your sex are personal *attributes*, elements of what you are as a person. Nobody chooses to be born black or white, male or female, and few can do anything to change these characteristics. In a liberal society grounded in the principle that individuals should be free to pursue happiness by developing their potential to the full, it is reasonable for the law to ensure that people's life chances are not stunted or privileged as a result of discrimination based on these elemental aspects of their identity.[22]

It could be argued that *age* is another 'basic role' (and indeed, Michael Banton identifies it as such), in which case, it too should be protected. But there are two key differences between age roles, and sex and race roles.

One is that we are not stuck in our age category. We change our ages over time, and all of us can expect to be young at one time, old at another. So if there are privileges or disadvantages associated with being young or old (e.g. young workers are paid less, or older workers must retire at 65), we will all experience them sooner or later, provided the rules don't change. Age discrimination is not, in this sense, 'unfair treatment' of any one set of people sharing an unalterable attribute, because we are all equally affected by the same rules (but at different times).

The second difference is that age has two aspects. One has to do with belonging to the younger or older generation; the other has to do with membership of a birth cohort. While all of us progress through different generational stages, from young to old, we all remain stuck in the cohort in which we happen to have been born, and some cohorts seem to enjoy more luck (or privileges) than others. Some endure wars; others don't. Some are afflicted with economic depressions; others enjoy long years of prosperity. Some enjoy generous welfare pay-outs; others end up paying higher taxes to finance the escalating welfare bills of previous cohorts.

This suggests that, if there is a case for anti-age discrimination legislation, it should aim at achieving fair and equal treatment between *cohorts* rather than between *generations*. There is, for example, a strong case for a law requiring governments to balance their current expenditure budgets over a business cycle so that one cohort does not get saddled with irresponsible debts racked up by another. Needless to say, no UK government has even thought about legislating on this.

Sometimes, what have been justified as anti-age discrimination measures turn out to be unfairly discriminatory between different cohorts. For example, abolition of the default retirement age has been justified on the grounds that it is wrong to discriminate against older workers. In reality, however, this change allows the current cohort of older workers to hang onto senior positions which the previous cohort (their parents' generation) were forced to relinquish to them. The baby boomer cohort has seized new advantages for itself which its parents did not enjoy, and it has imposed the costs of this change onto its children (for they must now wait longer before they can move into vacant leadership slots at the top of organisations).[23] The introduction of anti-age discrimination laws has therefore intensified unfair discrimination between cohorts.

Disability might also be thought to represent a 'basic role' that should be protected by anti-discrimination laws, but here too, the issue is not as simple as it might seem. There are three key differences between sex or race discrimination, and discrimination on the basis of disability.

First, while it is true that (as with sex and race) some people are born with a disability which they cannot do anything to change, this is not true of all disabled people. A smoker who develops emphysema, a cannabis user who becomes schizophrenic, or a chronically obese person who overeats and takes no exercise — all of these bear some responsibility for their circumstances as a result of their freely-chosen actions in the past.

The 2010 Equality Act explicitly excludes some self-inflicted disabilities (e.g. addiction to illegal substances) from protection, but many others are protected. But why should an employer, say, be required to ignore someone's acquired condition when deciding whether to offer them a job, or whether to dismiss them for taking too much time off work? If you bring about your own incapacity, why should others be required by law to incur unnecessary costs themselves in order to compensate for your acquired condition?

Secondly, disability can often be difficult to define or delimit, and the label covers a wide variety of conditions. About 18 per cent of the UK population (10 million people) claims to have a disability which is covered by anti-discrimination law, and more than 6.7 million of them are of working age.[24] When we read statistics like these, it is obvious that we are talking about a huge diversity of conditions. While some of these people are severely incapacitated, others can probably function for much of the time perfectly adequately, and some are simply masquerading or malingering, yet they all claim the same swathe of privileges and protections.[25]

Thirdly, and most pertinent for our present concerns, there is the problem that somebody's disability may be directly relevant to their suitability to perform the tasks for which the law is protecting them. Both the 1995 Disability Discrimination Act and the 2010 Equality Act allow employers to discriminate if someone's disability is 'material to the circumstances' of the job they are being asked to do (e.g. you can refuse to appoint someone in a wheelchair to a labouring job), although employers are required to make any 'reasonable adjustments' to accommodate disabled employees before rejecting them.

But the problem is that almost any serious disability will, by definition, impact on someone's ability to perform work tasks efficiently. This is precisely what 'disability' means. If you regularly have to take time off work, for example, you cannot perform the continuous and dependable functions required by most employers, yet an employer is not allowed to discriminate against you on these grounds. Making it unlawful to discriminate on grounds of disability means it can be unlawful to pick the most suitable person for the job.

Physical or mental disability is almost bound to impact on what people can do, and how well they can do it, for disability has to do with our *capacities* as much as our personal *attributes*. People's capacities are legitimate— indeed pressing—considerations for any employer. An employer who refuses to take on a black applicant may simply be bigoted, but an employer who refuses to take on someone whose chronic health problems mean they will have to take a lot of time off work might just be

38

trying to safeguard the reliability of the service their business provides.

What of *sexual orientation*? Somebody's sexuality is a key component of their sense of self, but unlike their sex or race, it is expressed through their *behaviour*, rather than being revealed in their physical *attributes*. This is why the Church, for example, has been able to accept gay men as priests on the condition that they remain celibate — the identity only becomes relevant in the behaviour.

One effect of this is that a person's sexuality will often not be apparent to other people unless he or she chooses to inform them of it. Many gay men and lesbians choose not to 'come out', which means their employers and others around them simply do not know what their sexuality is. When this is the case, their sexuality obviously remains irrelevant to the way they get treated. The same also applies to minority sexual tastes like cross-dressing.

Individuals have an absolute right to declare their sexuality, or to keep it private, whichever they prefer. It is their business. But if somebody exercises their right to declare themselves to be homosexual or transvestite, through what they say or the way they behave in public situations, other people presumably have an equivalent right to respond according to their own values and prejudices. It is one thing for the law to stop you discriminating against me because of what I am (a black person, a woman), but quite another for it to stop you discriminating against me because of what I do (my sexual behaviour). In a society which takes liberty seriously, my right to declare my gay pride must also imply your right to refuse to have anything to do with me.

Given that homosexual and transvestite identities are expressed in behaviour, it is difficult to see why this behavioural choice should be given any more legal protection than any other.[26] Why protect gays, but not Goths?[27] The Equality Act tacitly recognises this difficulty by explicitly excluding protection for people with other sexual tastes such as sado-masochism or paedophilia.[28] But given the logic of the legislation, provided such behaviour is legal and consensual, it is not clear why people with these preferences are not also included in the Act. If you give legal protection from discrimination to those who engage in homosexual acts, why not also protect leather fetishists, sado-masochists or pornography users? Conversely, if there is no case for special legal protections for these groups, then why gays?

There is, however, a complication in the argument that core attributes (race and sex) should be protected from discrimination, but behaviour (e.g. homosexuality) should not, and it arises in respect of the treatment of couples. Consider the case of a religious B&B proprietor who refuses to let a double room to a same-sex couple. We could argue that homosexual couples do not have to sleep together and that this problem therefore only arises because their expressed behavioural preference clashes with the behavioural rules laid down by the proprietor. On this logic, the B&B owner should be entitled to offer them separate rooms, or a room with twin beds, instead. But there is something wrong with this reasoning, as becomes clear if we apply the same logic to a mixed-race couple in the same situation. They too do not have to sleep together—it is their preference—yet we would surely resist the argument that guest houses should be allowed to enforce a miscegenation rule.

A guest house which refused to allow a mixed-race couple to share a bed would clearly be discriminating on the basis of race, even if it were willing to accommodate the two individuals in separate beds in a twin room, or in separate rooms. It would not be discriminating against the racial attributes of each individual (for it is happy to accommodate both of them), but it would be discriminating against the racial attributes of the couple (it will not accommodate them together). The same reasoning applies to discrimination against same-sex couples.

Neither partner in a gay couple is being discriminated against individually when they are refused a double room (for the guest house is perfectly happy to offer them a twin-bedded room or separate rooms), but they are experiencing illegitimate *sex discrimination* as a couple. If it is illegal to discriminate against individuals on the basis of their sex, then logically it must also be illegal to discriminate against couples on the basis of the sex of each partner. The issue is not one of sexual preference (the behaviour of the couple), but of sex (their gender attributes).

It follows that they should be protected from such discrimination, but this protection should be afforded under existing sex discrimination law. There should be no need for an additional law protecting sexual orientation.

The protection given to people with **religious or philosophical beliefs** is even more difficult to justify, for the public expression of beliefs is wholly voluntary. People may be born into a faith, or they may acquire it, but either way, it is nobody else's business unless they choose to make it so through proclamation, display or other actions. Once they do this, other people who share different beliefs, or none at all, must surely be free to exercise their choice as to whether they respond positively or negatively. If you do not want to risk negative responses from those who disagree or disapprove of your way of thinking, keep your beliefs to yourself.

The extension of legal protection to people with 'beliefs' opens all sorts of cans of worms when it comes to rights of free speech, and the courts and tribunals are likely to kept busy for many years trying to sort this out. Atheists, agnostics and humanists may seek protection under this legislation,[29] so the law has extended special protection to people with some views and ideologies, but not others. If I dislike David Cameron's views, I can refuse to employ him, or serve him in my business, but if I try to exclude Richard Dawkins or the Archbishop of Canterbury on the same grounds, I could be sued.

Extending protection from people's attributes to their beliefs also means that one set of protected characteristics may now clash directly with another. It is quite possible, for example, for a protected religious or philosophical group to hold beliefs which are discriminatory as regards another protected group. When this happens, the law gets itself into an awful pickle.

Many Christians and Muslims, for example, consider homosexuality to be sinful, but the Equality Act requires them to accept it. Christian B&B proprietors who refused to allow a gay couple to rent a double room were found to have acted unlawfully, and a black Pentecostal couple who had been fostering for 20 years were removed from the register because they believed homosexuality is sinful.[30] But aren't these religious beliefs themselves supposed to be protected? There is nothing in the law to explain why some protected groups should get more protection than others, and religious leaders have begun to complain that, in practice, equalities legislation is undermining religious liberties.[31]

How did we get here? Where are we going?

With the wisdom of hindsight, we can now see that sex and race were the Trojan horses of the equalities campaigners in the sixties and seventies. They were the areas where nobody could really object to anti-discrimination protections being offered by law. But once they were established, other, much weaker cases piled in behind. They were often driven on by impassioned activists determined that they should be afforded the same privileges, and they were acquiesced in by unprincipled politicians intent on currying favour with vociferous pressure groups, maximising votes and avoiding causing anybody any offence. Nobody really thought through what we were doing, or where we were going to end up. Even the 2010 Act, which was explicitly intended to rationalise all this legislation, failed to prompt any serious reflection by politicians. While the Labour Party presented itself as the champion of any 'oppressed' group that raised its hand, the Conservatives were scared of antagonising people by appearing to be 'the nasty party' opposed to 'equality'.

The result today is an unprincipled tangle of protections and entitlements which smother enterprise, strangle free speech, encourage rent seeking and special pleading on a huge scale and, in many cases, defy consistency or logic. Governments should have strong and compelling reasons for using the law to give special protection to certain sections of the population. I have suggested that these reasons exist in respect of people's basic attributes, the things they can do nothing to control or change, but that the grounds for protecting groups defined by their behaviour, their aptitudes or their attitudes and beliefs are much less compelling.

This does not mean people should not try to be pleasant, polite and tolerant of each other. They should. But in a grown-up, free society, the government should think twice before enforcing such behaviour with special laws, and we should all be cautious about the increasing use of law simply to safeguard people's feelings.

4

We are All Guilty

As well as extending the number of potential 'victim groups' which can claim protection, the development of equalities legislation since the 1970s has also stretched the definition of what constitutes 'unlawful' discrimination.

First, it introduced the idea of 'indirect discrimination', which holds that you may be discriminating unfairly against somebody even when you apply the same rules to them as to everybody else. Then it developed the idea of 'institutionalised' or 'systemic' discrimination, which means that you may be unfairly discriminating against somebody even if you have no intention of doing so and you bear them no malice or ill will. Finally, it ended up endorsing 'positive discrimination' (even though equalities campaigners still indignantly insist that no such thing exists in British law). This means that it is not unfair to discriminate against somebody provided you are helping someone else who belongs to a group which the government favours.

Indirect discrimination: it is not fair to apply the same rules to everyone

The 1975 Sex Discrimination Act marked an important watershed in equalities law, for not only did it extend existing protections enjoyed by ethnic minorities to women, but it also widened the concept of 'discrimination' to include 'indirect' as well as 'direct' forms. This redefinition was then reflected back into the race discrimination rules, and it has been extended into all the legislation that has followed, up to and including the 2010 Equality Act.

The 1975 Act made it illegal to discriminate against a female employee by treating her less favourably than a male in the same position. This is the familiar case of direct discrimination. But in addition, it also made it illegal for an employer to insist on any requirement or condition which was not strictly necessary in order to perform the task if fewer women than men would be able to meet this condition. This has become known as 'indirect discrimination'.[1]

For example, it would be illegal for an employer to require applicants for a job to meet certain physical strength requirements, unless they were genuinely required in order to perform the task. Such a requirement is not directly discriminatory, for it applies equally to male and female applicants, but it is indirectly discriminatory, because women are on average not as strong as men. Such a rule would tend to disadvantage female candidates, and would therefore be illegal.

Effectively, this new interpretation of discrimination made intention and motivation irrelevant. All that mattered now was whether women, on average, would be less likely to meet a given job requirement. Because women are more likely than men to take career breaks to raise children, employment tribunals have ruled against employers who have sought to link pay and employment conditions to length of service or age. Similarly, requiring employees to work antisocial hours can put a company in breach of the sex discrimination laws, because women often have family responsibilities which prevent them from working late. Even insisting that workers should be willing to relocate can be deemed discriminatory, because women may be less able to move home, given that many households rely mainly on a male partner's income.[2]

Despite its problems, this new concept of indirect discrimination was swiftly extended to racial equality law. In 1976, a new Race Relations Act updated the 1965 and 1968 Acts to bring them into line with the recent sex equality legislation. The Race Relations Board, which had been created under the 1965 legislation, was replaced by a new Commission for Racial Equality, with similar powers and functions to those of the Equal Opportunities Commission, and the definition of racial discrimination was extended to include indirect as well as direct forms.

The key wording in the 1976 Race Relations Act was almost identical to that in the 1975 Sex Discrimination Act. It outlawed 'less favourable treatment' on grounds of race (direct discrimination), and it banned the application of any unnecessary requirement or condition where the proportion of people from one ethnic group who are able to comply is less than that from another (indirect discrimination). For example, it became unlawful for an employer to ban employees from wearing headgear, since this rule works to the disadvantage of Sikhs wearing turbans. On the same reasoning, it has recently been ruled that schools cannot ban cornrow hairstyles as this indirectly discriminates against Afro-Caribbean pupils.[3] Local authorities and housing associations have been prevented from favouring locally-born families when allocating public housing, for this indirectly discriminates against people born overseas.

As later legislation extended protections to more groups, so the prohibition on indirect as well as direct discrimination has been reproduced almost word for word in each new Act and statutory instrument. As a result, today, it is not only unlawful to treat people differently on grounds of their race, sex, religion, sexuality and so on, but in each case it is also unlawful to adopt any rules or procedures which may place one group at a disadvantage relative to another.

This extension of equalities law to cover indirect discrimination represents a major shift, for it turns the definition of discrimination into a test of statistical probabilities rather than a matter of intentional exclusion. For example, an employment tribunal ruled in 2002 that a company which limited applications for a new high-level post to staff currently occupying higher-grade positions had acted unlawfully, because there were no black African employees in higher positions. The selection criterion therefore made it impossible for any black Africans in the company to apply for the post.[4] It was clearly not the intention of this company to discriminate against black Africans. Ironically, the post in question was that of Equal Opportunities Manager, and the company wanted to limit applications to senior staff precisely because it intended the new position to be powerful and to be taken seriously by others in the company. Nevertheless, the unintended effect of its job specifications was still held to be discriminatory.

When we have got to the point where a company which is trying to strengthen its anti-discrimination procedures is found to have been discriminatory in the way it was going about it, we can be pretty sure that Alice's Wonderland is just around the next corner. The problems arise because human intention and motivation are no longer the issue. All that matters is outcomes.

From 1975 onwards, it has been possible for someone to discriminate illegally against someone else on the grounds of their sex or race (and later, various other protected characteristics), even if they had no idea that this is what they were doing. It was but a short step from here to the discovery of 'institutional' racism, sexism, disabilism and homophobia, where the question of how individuals behave becomes entirely irrelevant.

Institutionalised discrimination: your motives and intentions are irrelevant

The concept of 'institutional racism' first emerged in America in the 1960s when the militant Black Power and anti-Semitic activist, Stokely Carmichael, used it to describe the treatment of blacks in the Southern USA. Importantly, as Norman Dennis notes,[5] Carmichael was writing in a context where blacks had for a century been oppressed by blatantly racist laws and public policies which excluded them from white schools, barred them from white shops and restaurants, and classified them as inferior citizens. What Carmichael was referring to, therefore, was the way racist beliefs and attitudes were not only expressed by many southern white individuals at that time, but were inscribed in core social institutions of the Deep South such as the police, the schools and the churches. It was a powerful and undeniable claim.

When racism is inscribed within organisational rules and practices in this way, it may not matter very much whether the individuals working within these organisations themselves hold racist views. To take an example offered by Dennis, the segregated public transport laws in Alabama meant that bus drivers had to tell black passengers like Rosa Parks to occupy the rear seats, irrespective of their own views on the matter. Non-racist drivers could comply with the rule, or they could resign. Those who stayed in their jobs and implemented the policy were still morally responsible, of course, but any explanation of their actions would be incomplete without reference to the institutional context in which they were operating.

Understood in this way, there is no reason why 'institutional racism' should not in principle be observed and measured in empirical research. We can study the rule books of organisations; we can interview the owners and managers of businesses; we can observe what happens if people from ethnic minorities try to use services which have been deliberately set up to exclude them. This, however, is not the way the concept is being used today.

The key change in the official understanding of what is entailed by 'institutional' exclusion came about as a result of the hugely influential Macpherson Inquiry into the murder of Stephen Lawrence in 1993. Stephen Lawrence was a black teenager who was stabbed by a gang of white youths while he was waiting for a bus with a friend in South London one April evening. The Metropolitan Police later arrested five white youths who had a history of violence (against whites as well as blacks), but the Crown Prosecution Service advised that the evidence was not strong enough to prosecute them. Against the advice of the police, the Lawrence family then brought their own private prosecution, but crucial identification evidence was deemed inadmissible, and the judge instructed the jury to find the defendants not guilty. The family, who believed that a racist police force had failed to investigate their son's murder properly, then took their grievances to the Police Complaints Authority. It investigated their claims and concluded that, notwithstanding various oversights and omissions during the investigation of the murder, there was no evidence to support their allegation of racist misconduct. There had been incompetence, to be sure, but it had nothing to do with racism.

There the matter rested until the newly elected Blair government decided to set up a full public inquiry, chaired by Sir William Macpherson.[6] Macpherson's inquiry abandoned many of the traditional features of English law. Witnesses were harassed, not only by the inquiry team, but by the crowd in the public gallery. They were asked to admit to having had 'racist thoughts', and even to testify to the existence of racist thoughts among their colleagues. Norman Dennis likens the proceedings to a Stalinist show trial from the 1930s.

Despite his unusual methods, Macpherson found no evidence of racism on the part of individual police officers. Nor did he find any evidence of established rules and procedures within the police force which operated to the disadvantage of blacks or other ethnic minorities. But in the end, none of this mattered, for following the advice of various radical academics and activists who gave 'evidence' to the inquiry, Macpherson extended the definition of 'institutional racism' to include what Dennis calls 'racism that cannot be seen, that cannot be proven'.[7]

According to the Macpherson Report, institutional racism involves 'processes, attitudes and behaviour which amount to discrimination through unwitting prejudice, ignorance, thoughtlessness and racist stereotyping which disadvantage minority ethnic people. It persists because of the failure of the organisation openly and adequately to recognise and address its existence and causes by policy, example and leadership.'[8] And on this definition, Macpherson found the Metropolitan Police (and British society as a whole) guilty as charged.

Macpherson thought this hidden form of institutional racism manifested itself in the fact that the police had initially failed to recognise the Stephen Lawrence murder as 'purely racially motivated' (given that the suspects had also perpetrated violence against white victims, this reluctance to jump to conclusions may have been understandable). He also pointed to national stop and search statistics which showed that the police stop a disproportionate number of black youths. Macpherson thought this indicated 'racist stereotyping' by officers, but as we shall see in chapter 9, black youths are actually stopped in proportion to their presence on the streets. The fact that ethnic minorities often say they do not trust the police, that blacks were 'under-represented' among recruits to the Met, and that the police were not routinely subjected to race awareness training, were also all taken by Macpherson as indirect evidence that the force was 'infected' with racism.

Basically, what Macpherson was saying was that any black/white differences in policing and the law and order system more generally pointed to the existence of institutional racism. There was no need to investigate motives, intentions, behaviour or rules and procedures; all that mattered was *outcomes*. If black people have a problem, it must be due to racism, and if white police officers deny it, this is further evidence of their own failure to acknowledge the problem.

As we shall see in chapter 7, Macpherson's legacy has turned logic on its head. If we find, for example, that blacks are over-represented in the arrest statistics, or the prison statistics, we no longer even ask whether this might be because they commit more crimes per head of population than whites do. Rather, since Macpherson, we take these outcomes to be the product of the institutional racism which we 'already know' pervades the criminal justice system. Yet the only evidence we have that this 'racism' even exists is that outcomes like these can be found. The argument is therefore entirely circular and is immune to disconfirmation.

Once we start out with the assumption that the Metropolitan Police (or any other agency) is institutionally racist, it becomes impossible to disprove it.[9] I call this form of reasoning the 'fallacy of proportionate outcomes,' for it rests on the unacknowledged and implausible assumption that all outcomes would be the same for all social groups in all areas of life were it not for the operation of institutional bias.

One consequence of this terrifying logic has been the abandonment of the principle of formal equality in the way the police are now trained to deal with incidents involving ethnic minorities. Back in the sixties, when campaigners first started agitating to end racial discrimination, their aim was to achieve a 'colour-blind' application of policies and procedures by all relevant agencies. The belief was that the police, for example, should apply the law, without fear or favour, regardless of whether the perpetrator or the victim was black or white. Post-Macpherson, however, this laudable commitment to formal equality has been shredded.

David Green quotes from the Association of Chief Police Officers' *Hate Crime Manual*: '"Colour-blind" policing means policing that purports to treat everyone in the same way. Such an approach is flawed and unjust... There was a time when to be passively non-racist was considered sufficient (i.e. the passive state of expressing no prejudice and engaging in no racially discriminatory behaviours). This is not enough. In a passively non-racist environment, racists can still thrive, discriminatory organisational structures and practices can still persist, and racism in the broader community can go largely unchallenged.'[10] We have, in other words, now reached a point where police officers are being instructed by those in command to treat ethnic minorities differently from whites. And this is being done in the name of 'equality'.

It is not only in policing that discrimination is said to have become 'institutionalised'. Macpherson declared that: 'It is clear that other agencies including those for example dealing with housing and education also suffer from the disease.'[11] And so it is that in recent years, the BBC has been attacked by a former Director General for being 'hideously white'; museums and art galleries have been criticised by an ex-minister for being 'too white'; and a former Chair of the Mental Health Act Commission has accused the mental health sector of being 'institutionally racist'. As Munira Mirza (who reports these three examples) points out: 'In this new approach, no one and everyone is guilty of racism. Any unequal outcome is assumed to be the result of prejudice.'[12]

Nor is the problem of institutionalised prejudice any longer limited to issues of race. In 2009, the NHS was reported to be 'institutionally ageist' because younger patients are sometimes given higher priority for treatment than older sufferers.[13] Wherever statistical differences can be found, accusations of systemic bias can be raised, which is why today we increasingly hear claims of this or that institution being inherently sexist, ageist, homophobic or even disabilist. Once the need to prove intention, motivation or even conscious awareness is removed, it becomes open season for the equalities industry to attack all the core institutions of our society, and that is exactly what they have been doing.

Positive discrimination: It's OK to discriminate against white, middle-class, heterosexual males

After being battered into accepting that our institutions are 'systemically biased' against minority groups, all that remains is to counter this bias by setting up rules and procedures which deliberately and flagrantly favour those whom we believe to be disadvantaged. Today's institutional racism gives rise to tomorrow's positive discrimination.

Positive discrimination first appeared in UK law in 1995 when the Disability Discrimination Act made it unlawful for employers, shops, local authorities and other organisations to fail to make 'reasonable adjustments' to accommodate the needs of disabled people. This was the first time that British equalities law established a positive duty to do something specifically designed to benefit a protected group. The definition of a 'reasonable adjustment' has been honed by subsequent tribunals, but it includes making physical alterations to premises, amending employees' duties or working hours, modifying equipment, providing special training, and organising helpers or specialist supervision.[14] Where adjustments would be very costly, or would create problems for other users, they may not be regarded as reasonable.

This positive duty to do something to bring about a 'fairer' outcome, created in 1995 in the case of disability, was extended in the Race Relations (Amendment) Act of 2000, which introduced a new duty on public bodies to promote racial equality. The 2006 Equality Act then extended this to sex equality by imposing a 'gender duty' on public bodies to actively promote equality between the sexes. Finally, in 2010, all the other protected groups got brought under this umbrella too. And there is the prospect of imposing something similar on private firms too.

The law and guidelines on positive discrimination have become hopelessly muddled as a result of these developments. It looks very much as if politicians want to encourage managers and administrators to bias their procedures in favour of selected victim groups, but they don't yet feel they can admit this is what is going on.

The obfuscation began under the last Labour government. Responding to the Macpherson Report, Home Office Minister Mike O'Brien defended the introduction of 'targets' for ethnic minority recruitment into the police force, but denied that this entailed imposition of 'quotas'. 'Quotas,' he explained, 'are illegal... Targets are about fairness, rewarding talent and putting an end to glass ceilings. Managers will have to deliver their targets.' This was, as David Green suggests, 'sheer doubletalk,' for if managers are to be judged on whether they meet their targets, this must entail the use of quotas and a corresponding move away from purely meritocratic appointment procedures. How else could they ensure that targets will be met?[15]

This sort of duplicity has continued under the Coalition government. Since April 2011, as a result of the implementation of the 2010 Equality Act, employers have been permitted 'to apply voluntary positive action in recruitment and promotion processes when faced with two or more candidates of equal merit, to address under-representation in the workforce'.[16] The government insists that this does not imply quotas, and that 'positive discrimination is not acceptable and is unlawful'.[17] So employers are being encouraged to 'apply positive action' to increase the number of people they employ with protected characteristics, but they must not engage in 'positive discrimination'.

Critics describe this hair-splitting as 'Soviet-style doublespeak' and say that what is really being instituted is a new policy which allows people to be offered a job on the grounds of their race, sex, religion, sexuality or age.[18] Defenders of the policy struggle to counter such claims. Bob Fahy, for example, insists that critics are wrong when they say that positive discrimination is now sanctioned in law: 'Positive discrimination, per se, has never been, and is not now, lawful under UK employment law'.[19] But he then adds three provisos in swift succession:

- 'except perhaps in the field of disability discrimination, where there can be positive obligations to make reasonable adjustments...';

- 'even before the Equality Act came into force, positive action was permitted... to provide support (such as additional training) to under-represented groups and to encourage the take-up of jobs'; and

- 'the key change introduced by the [2010] Act has been the introduction of a tie-breaker provision which essentially provides that if two candidates for promotion of recruitment are equally qualified for a position, the potential employer may select the candidate who has a protecting characteristic.'

Fahy denies all of this adds up to positive discrimination because 'no obligation is imposed on employers' to select minority candidates, but this is clearly a fallacious argument. There is no obligation on employers to be unfair to women, ethnic minorities or other protected groups, but this does not mean there is no 'negative discrimination' against these groups. By the same token, the absence of a requirement to discriminate positively does not mean this is not going to happen as a result of setting targets. The argument is clearly specious.

The government denies it is setting quotas, yet it proudly boasts of having 'set a new aspiration that 50 per cent of all new appointments to public boards will be women'.[20] Ministers are also happy to set 'targets' for ethnic minority recruitment into the police, or selection of students from poor backgrounds into Oxbridge. Yet they continue to deny that this is the same as establishing 'quotas'. Quotas, they insist, are illegal, yet targets are mandatory. It takes a particular kind of political intelligence to discern the difference.

5

One Law for You, Another for Me

In the 1990s, equalities legislation was pushed in yet another fresh direction as Parliament legislated to outlaw 'hate crimes' while judges began to get more involved in determining where 'social justice' lies. The result has been a disturbing shift away from the key principle of any liberal society that everyone should be treated equally under the same laws.

A special kind of victim

Ever since 1965, race has been a special area of the law when it comes to the right to free speech. Before 1965 the law prohibited any speech or behaviour likely to cause a breach of the peace, but the 1965 Race Discrimination Act added a specific, new criminal offence of incitement of racial hatred. This was later incorporated into the 1986 Public Order Act, and has subsequently been extended to include incitement to religious hatred, and hatred of gay men, lesbians and bisexuals.

Ever since 1965, therefore, we have been using the law to stop people influencing what other people think (not just what other people do). By making incitement of racial hatred a distinct type of offence, Parliament outlawed any use of words that a court could consider likely to stir up negative *emotions* about racial minorities (and later, other protected groups). It does not matter if the words used have no impact on people's subsequent behaviour; it is

59

enough that they foment hatred in people's minds. This is what Orwell called 'thought crime'.

This singling out of race as deserving of special treatment under the law was pushed a hefty step further in 1998 when the Crime and Disorder Act introduced the concept of 'racially aggravated offences'.[1] Prompted partly by the Stephen Lawrence case, this new law identified a number of offences, including assault, harassment, criminal damage and public order offences, which could now be punished more severely if they are found to have been motivated by racial animosity. The normal maximum sentence for common assault, for example, is six months, but racially aggravated common assault can attract a two-year term in prison. The minimum term usually served for murder is 15 years, but with racial aggravation, this stretches to 30.[2]

As is common in equalities legislation, once this innovation had been made in respect of one group, it swiftly got extended to others. In 2001, following pressure from Muslim activists, the Anti-Terrorism Act extended the special legal protection of ethnic minorities to religious groups by outlawing 'religiously-aggravated crimes'. Two years after that, the 2003 Criminal Justice Act required that courts regard as an 'aggravating factor' evidence that any offence was motivated by 'hostility' based on disability or sexual orientation. The result is that we now live in a country where you can be punished differently for the same action depending on the identity of your victim.

If you are black and are attacked by a white person, for example, your attacker may be punished more severely than if he or she was black. Similarly, if you are Muslim and are assaulted by a Christian, or you are homosexual and your property is criminally damaged by heterosexuals, or you are disabled and find yourself harassed by people who have no disability, you can claim to have been the victim of a hate crime, and if found guilty, your assailant will be punished more heavily than would otherwise have been the case. Hate crimes legislation therefore encourages some offences to be treated more seriously than others by the police and the courts, simply on the basis of the victim's identity.

Hate crime is everywhere!

All of this raises the tricky question of how the police are to determine whether a crime was motivated by racism, homophobia, dislike of disabled people, religious hatred, or whatever. The answer is that an offence is a hate crime if the victim (or anybody else) thinks it is.

The Macpherson report is partly to blame for this extraordinary lapse into subjectivism, for it explicitly recommended that the police should treat any incident as racist if it 'is perceived to be racist by the victim or any other person'.[3] This means that anyone with a chip on their shoulder has to be taken seriously, and woe betide any police officer who uses their discretion or common sense to come to an alternative interpretation of the case before them. As the Association of Chief Police Officers explains: 'To report or record an incident as racist or homophobic, *evidence is not needed*. Evidence is not the test. Perception on the part of anyone is all that is required.'[4] As a result of Macpherson's advice, the Crown Prosecution Service (CPS) also now defines a racist incident as 'any incident that is perceived to be racist by the victim or any other person'.[5] Similarly, by extension, the CPS advises that homophobic incidents and

Islamaphobic incidents are those perceived to be such by the victim or any other party.

Not surprisingly, given this latitude, the number of 'hate crimes' and 'hate incidents' has risen dramatically since they were first recognised in UK law. In 1998, when the Crime and Disorder Act created the category of 'racially-aggravated offences', 1,602 people were charged with racist crimes.[6] By 2005, this had risen almost five-fold, to 7,430. In that year, it also became possible to commit a religiously-aggravated crime, so the total number of hate crimes that got prosecuted rose to 8,868. By 2009, this combined figure had increased to 11,624, but by then, sexuality, transgender and disability had been added to the list, so a further 1,406 people were prosecuted for homophobic or disability-related offences.

The numbers have been further ramped up by the creation of special CPS Hate Crime Scrutiny Panels, which have been operating since 2004.[7] They are made up of representatives of 'victim groups' across all 42 areas of the CPS, and their job is to encourage alleged 'victims' to bring complaints. According to Green, this means they effectively go on 'fishing expeditions', and the police are increasingly pushed into defining relatively trivial incidents as hate crimes.

This pressure to keep finding, reporting and prosecuting real or imagined examples of hate crime is further reinforced by equalities campaigners who complain that many such crimes are still going unreported. In its recent report, *How Fair is Britain?*, for example, the EHRC blithely accepts an estimate by the gay pressure group, Stonewall, that two-thirds of gay men, lesbians and bisexual people experienced a 'homophobic crime or incident' between 2005 and 2008.[8]

It further estimates that three in four people who experience 'homophobic hate crime' fail to report it.[9]

There is, of course, no way of assessing the validity of estimates like these. By conflating 'crimes' (breaches of the criminal law) with 'incidents' (anything a person chooses to define as relevant), Stonewall manages to generate huge, yet utterly meaningless, numbers. According to the British Crime Survey, only one in a thousand gay/lesbian/bisexual people say they have been the victim of a hate crime in the previous 12 months.[10] Yet despite reporting this much more modest statistic, the EHRC dutifully and uncritically reproduces Stonewall's claims, and then goes on to flag the reduction of 'hate crimes' as one of its 'key priorities'.

Depressingly, the new Coalition government enthusiastically goes along with this nonsense in its Equality Strategy. It promises to 'promote better recording of all hate crimes, but particularly those which at present are not centrally recorded, for example against disabled people and LGB&T people,' and it promises to 'encourage those who experience hate crime to report it'.[11] The numbers, therefore, are almost bound to keep increasing in the future, and the more they spiral, the more we will be told how much we need all this special legislation and protection.

It is not just the police who are caught in this web. Ever since the 2000 Race Relations (Amendment) Act, all public bodies have been under a duty to 'promote race equality', and one result of this is that all schools are now required to refer any 'racist incidents' to local authorities and to keep a record of all such occurrences. Because the definition of a 'racist incident' is vague and broad, schools tend to err on the side of caution and report even the most trifling incidents. Indeed, schools which make nil returns are criticised for 'under-reporting'.[12]

The predictable result has been an avalanche of a quarter of a million 'racist incidents' being reported by schools between 2002 and 2009. In 2008-09, more than thirty thousand 'racist incident' reports were lodged with local authorities in England and Wales, and in more than half of these cases, the perpetrators were of primary school age (there were even 40 incidents reported by nursery schools).[13] The great majority of cases were trivial (95 per cent involved verbal abuse or name-calling), but once a school has reported an incident, the police feel they have to invest it with due seriousness, and the rest of the criminal justice system then grinds into action behind them.

In 2007-08, the Crown Prosecution Service prosecuted 2,916 children aged between 10 and 17 for race or religious hate crimes (up from 404 two years earlier), and 350 primary school pupils were suspended or expelled for racist abuse. According to the Manifesto Club, a civil liberties group: 'Such anti-racist policies can create divisions where none had existed, by turning everyday playground spats into race issues... most of these "racist incidents" are just kids falling out.'[14]

Yet again, one is put in mind of the seventeenth century witchcraft trials in Europe. Once an agency has it fixed in its thinking that a problem exists, it finds examples of it everywhere, and the more action it takes to stamp it out, the more examples keep cropping up. The last time we went through something like this, a lot of people got burned before we finally came to our senses.

The law as a political instrument

One of the things that happens when the law starts to give special recognition to particular sections of the population is that there is a clamour among individuals to get themselves re-classified into one of the favoured identity groups. David Green refers to this process as 'category creep', and he suggests it has gone furthest in 'disability'. He notes that in the USA, alcoholics and obese people have succeeded in getting themselves included in disabilities legislation, and in the UK too, the 2010 Equality Act covers discrimination against 'clinically obese' people.

Another thing that happens when the law starts to be subverted in this way is that sections of the population which manage to get themselves officially recognised as 'protected' start to use their legally privileged status to consolidate their own privileges and to silence potential adversaries. They are able to do this because once a group is 'protected' it becomes difficult for others to challenge its activities or question its claims. This is particularly pernicious in the case of religious and philosophical groups which can gain effective immunity from challenge in open debate and argument, but it also has unfortunate consequences for anyone opposing groups with protected lifestyles. Thus, anyone who criticises, say, Islamic beliefs, or who questions homosexual adoption, is immediately marginalised and labelled as 'oppressive'. The substance of their argument is pushed to one side; the mere fact that they are challenging a protected group is enough to drown out their views, and (as Christian B&B owners found in 2009 when they criticised the faith of a Muslim guest) it may even put them on the wrong side of the law.[15] As Green suggests: 'Any criticism is "blaming the victim"... the process resembles the invention of permanent victimhood, captured by words such as Islamophobia, homophobia and disabilism.'[16]

This closing down of debate and insulation of special interests from the kind of criticism and questioning that commonly applies to everyone else is clearly inimical to the English liberal tradition. In his celebrated essay, *On Liberty*, the nineteenth century liberal philosopher John Stuart Mill emphasised the importance of free and open thought and discussion, not just as a precondition of the exercise of individual freedom, but also because we can never be sure that one opinion is valid and another is false. Even the most plausible and attractive contentions need constantly to be challenged if they are to remain vital and avoid the 'deep slumber of a decided opinion'.[17] For Mill, therefore, the law should never be used to close down critical discussion, and there is no justification for shutting people up just to protect the feelings of others. He insisted that governments should resist the temptation to use their powers to support one moral standpoint against another, and that the law must stand above mere sectional disputes rather than taking sides.

Today, a century-and-a-half after that essay was written, Mill's warnings go unheeded, and his principle of liberty lies in tatters. Vociferous interest groups have pushed supine politicians into awarding them a privileged political status which has placed them above the rough-and-tumble of debate and argument. As David Green suggests, this has changed the way our legal system works, for the old principle that all individuals are equal under the law has been supplanted by the recognition of certain group identities as deserving of special treatment. Where the principle of formal equality required abstract rules to govern the relations between people in a neutral and detached way, equalities law now deliberately engineers outcomes so they will favour one group over another.

Power to the judges

Recent equalities legislation, and especially the 2010 Equality Act, has also shifted more power into the hands of the judiciary. This is partly because judges have inevitably been called upon to try to sort out the tangle of competing rights and claims which the new laws have created. When, for example, the rights of a Christian couple to have their religious beliefs respected clashed with the rights of a gay couple to book a double room in their B&B, it fell to the judges to decide whose rights should prevail (in this case, the judges decided that gay rights trump Christian rights).[18]

The empowerment of the judges reflects more than simply the complexity of our current legislation, however. It seems to have been deliberately engineered by the last Labour government. Perhaps recognising that the judiciary has been moving leftwards in its inclinations and sympathies, ministers created a constitutional barrier to any possible back-sliding by future administrations by imposing 'equality audits' on all future legislation. Equalities law requires government ministers to check, before implementing any new policy, that their decisions will not 'unfairly' impact on any of the groups with 'protected characteristics'. In this way, equalities law sets limits to any other policies that might be mooted across the whole range of government—equality is trumps.

As a result of this requirement, ministers in the Coalition government that followed Labour into power in 2010 have reportedly been left helpless in the hands of their departmental legal advisers. The *Spectator* reported in 2011 that whenever ministers try to implement an agreed policy, they get warned that they are on 'unsound legal ground'.[19] Harriett Harman, the former Equalities Minister who ushered the Equality Bill through Parliament in the dying days of the Brown government, effectively hobbled her Tory successors, and the Conservatives then paid the price for not having opposed the Bill when it was going through the Commons.[20] 'You can in theory defy the lawyer,' one minister is quoted as saying, 'but if you spent tens of thousands of pounds on a legal action which you then lost, and it emerged that you were advised not to fight, you would be in an awkward position.'[21]

The equalities and diversity lobby is increasingly aware of the potential uses of this power which the 2010 Act has dropped into their laps. When the new Coalition government introduced its first budget in June 2010, for example, the EHRC warned the Treasury that it could be in breach of the 2006 Equality Act, for public spending cuts would affect the poor more than the rich, and the Act requires all public bodies to have 'due regard' to the impact of their decisions on social inequality.[22]

The Fawcett Society (which campaigns on gender equality) went further. It brought an action in the High Court seeking a judicial review on the grounds that Treasury had failed to consider the impact of the proposed spending cuts on the nine protected groups, as it is required to do under the Equality Act. This action failed, but subsequent challenges have met with more success. In January 2011, the High Court overturned planned cuts of £10 million in council grants to voluntary organisations in London on the grounds that the local authorities concerned had not produced full equality impact assessments before ordering the cuts, and were therefore in breach of their statutory equality duties. Left activists began speculating that legal challenges like this might be an effective weapon in their fight against the policies of the elected government in Westminster.[23]

It is not only British judges who have been empowered by the extension of equalities legislation. The judges on the European Court increasingly intervene as well. In February 2011, for example, a Belgian consumer group appealed to the European Court of Justice to outlaw the use of gender to calculate car insurance premiums.[24] Women, on average, have fewer and less expensive accidents than men, so their premiums have historically been lower. But the European Court ruled that this is in breach of the EU equality laws set out in the Charter of Fundamental Rights, which formed part of the Lisbon Treaty. As a result, women drivers in Britain must now pay the same premiums as men, even though they tend to be safer. This ruling has also meant that insurance companies can no longer offer higher annuity rates to men (even though they tend to die earlier, and therefore claim less on average than women do). All such risk pooling—the very essence of insurance—has now been ruled illegal.

6

The Equalities Industry

How many people are employed to look out for all the inequalities which have now been made illegal? And how much does all this cost?

Aboard the spaceship **Golgafrincham**

At one point in their travels through the Universe, Arthur Dent, Ford Prefect, Zaphod Beeblebrox and the other characters in Douglas Adams's *Hitchhiker's Guide to the Galaxy* series teleport aboard the spaceship Golgafrincham, which they find filled with the cryogenically frozen bodies of telephone sanitisers, advertising account executives, and other people trained in skills of dubious social utility. They are told by the Captain that the ship had been launched long ago from a doomed planet to colonise a new home. But it soon becomes clear that these people's home planet was not really doomed, and that everybody aboard the Golgafrincham has been hood-winked by the more useful people on their planet into believing they had to leave while everyone else stayed behind. While they float aimlessly through space on a never-ending trip to nowhere, the rest of the population back home is happily getting on with their productive lives.

Had Arthur and his companions searched the ship more thoroughly, they might have found, deep in the hold, a pod containing the frozen bodies of thousands of equality and diversity officers.

Every time new equalities laws and regulations have been introduced by governments, thousands of new jobs in 'equality and diversity' management and administration have been created. Today, equality and diversity is a thriving industry providing secure and attractive employment for thousands of non-productive people. In 2009, the industry even spawned its own professional body to represent its interests, the Institute of Equality and Diversity Practitioners.[1]

Despite a deep recession and escalating unemployment, an online vacancy search will in any week turn up many attractive vacancies in this industry. The jobs are scattered through both the public and private sectors. For example:[2]

- The 'Equality Challenge Unit', which advises UK universities, has launched 'an ambitious three year strategic plan' for which it needs to appoint two new Senior Policy Advisers (one to work on religion and belief and sexual orientation equality, and the other to work on race equality) at a starting salary of £36,166 each, as well as a Research and Data Officer, at £32,000. All these posts offer a final salary pension scheme, plus 31 days annual holiday (in addition to public holidays).

- A global legal firm based in London wants to recruit a Head of Diversity and Inclusion 'to take an integral role in shaping and driving forward the firm's inclusivity agenda and programme'. It is offering a salary between £90,000 and £120,000 per annum.

- A City-based financial services company is advertising for a Diversity Manager at a salary of between £55,000 and £65,000 per year. The successful candidate will 'take a lead in implementing the

Gender Action Plan (GAP) increasing the economic participation of women'.

- A housing association, based in Kent, needs a Diversity Manager to 'provide expertise in the field of Diversity' and to 'mainstream equalities into service provision as appropriate'. For this, it is offering a salary of £30,000. The job advert warns that the successful candidate should be willing to 'attend meetings, seminars and conferences'.

- The Nursing and Midwifery Council seeks a Head of Equality and Inclusion whose job will be to 'research and monitor the diversity of the nurses and midwives on the register'. It promises a 'competitive salary'.

Cast around on the internet and you will find hundreds of similar advertisements for equality and diversity administrators, secretaries, managers, officers, consultants, specialists and researchers.[3] The equalities industry appears to be recession-proof, for even when the economy contracts and the public sector has to tighten its belt, statutory reporting requirements mean that equality and diversity staff still have to be retained. Local authorities may be closing libraries and shutting Sure Start centres, but they dare not think of touching their equality and diversity units.

The astounding thing about the growth of this industry is that none of these people produces anything that other people want to buy. They are only employed because equalities legislation requires companies and public sector agencies to monitor what they are doing and to report on the way they do it. The people who are employed to do this monitoring and write these reports produce nothing of value themselves (the only people who are interested in the reports they produce are other employees of the equalities industry sitting in other offices), so the costs of employing them—their salaries, their pensions, their office space, their conferences—all have to be passed on, either to customers (through higher prices) or to taxpayers.

'Savings' from increased equality

The thousands of people employed in this new equalities industry are, in economists' jargon, classic 'rent seekers'. They produce nothing, but live off the revenues generated by productive workers. But officials, academics and pressure groups associated with the Equalities Industry naturally deny this. They claim that, far from costing money, equalities legislation actually *saves* the country billions of pounds.

The TUC, for example, claims that discrimination against women workers is costing the economy £11 billion each year in under-utilisation of human capital.[4] The more diversity officers we employ, the more we can presumably whittle down this huge bill.

The Coalition government also uses these sorts of arguments. Its 2010 Equalities Strategy uncritically reported a National Audit Office estimate that discrimination against ethnic minorities costs the economy £8.6 billion every year in wasted talent. Note, incidentally, the claim to scientific precision implied by that decimal point. The intended message is that these are carefully-calibrated estimates, accurate to the nearest hundred thousand pounds.

The Coalition's Equalities Strategy also cites a Women and Work Commission estimate that eliminating gender segregation (i.e. getting women to do the same jobs as men in the same numbers) and increasing women's employment (i.e. getting women who prefer to be housewives or to work part-time to go to work full-time instead) 'could be worth about £15 billion to £23 billion to the economy each year'. Eliminating violence against women would save us even more: £37.6 billion (note the decimal point again) annually.[5]

Add this lot up, and we are being told that, if only we were 'fairer' to women and ethnic minorities, the economy would be almost £60 billion richer every year. And this is just the start! The National Skills Forum says that raising the rate of employment of disabled people to the national average would boost the UK economy by £13 billion every year.[6] And according to the Employers Forum on Age, age discrimination in employment costs the UK economy a whopping £31 billion per year.[7] Add these figures into the mix and we get to more than £100 billion—around seven per cent of GDP, or one-seventh of everything central and local government spends in an entire year.

This is a huge sum, and it almost completely eclipses the comparatively trifling amounts the equalities legislation costs us. It is very difficult to estimate how many people are directly employed in the equalities industry, but 35,000 individuals have registered to receive *Equality News*, the EHRC's monthly e-bulletin, so presumably most of them have an active professional interest in this field. If we make an initial and very crude assumption that all of these people work in equalities-related jobs (as academics, researchers, administrators or managers) at an average cost of £50,000 each, this would still add up to less than £2 billion each year. So for an outlay of under £2 billion, we get £100 billion back. What a bargain![8]

In reality, of course, most estimates of the benefits to be derived from equality and diversity legislation are meaningless. They are usually generated by throwing a few income statistics into a multiple regression equation, turning the handle, and seeing what comes out the other end.

Take that £15 to £23 billion 'saving' from eliminating gender inequalities in the workplace. It has been calculated by working out how much extra output would be generated in the economy if women were doing the same jobs as men, paid at the same rate, and if they participated in the labour market in the same proportions as men. But as we shall see in chapter 8, these assumptions ignore all the evidence on what men and women actually want in the way of employment. Most men and women do not *want* to work in the same jobs, and only a minority of women want to devote their lives to building careers (even though the equalities industry thinks they all should). It is not inequality that is preventing this from happening; it is people's preferences.

The only way to generate the 'savings' of £15 to £23 billion that the Equalities Strategy refers to would be to force millions of women to do science rather than arts degrees, to take private sector rather than public sector jobs, to work as software engineers and architects, rather than as teachers and vets, and to put their children in nurseries and crèches even if they prefer to spend time with them at home. These estimates, in other words, belong in the Utopian world of the all-knowing and all-powerful central planner, directing human resources to the economic niches where they can most efficiently be deployed, but completely ignoring what flesh-and-blood human beings actually want to do with their lives.

Even in the imaginary world of the Utopian central planner, moreover, efficiency savings of £15 to £23 billion would still not eventuate. As one critic of all this nonsense recently pointed out, estimates like this take no account of the fact that, if all this 'wasted' female labour were drafted into work, total labour supply would rise dramatically, wages would fall, and many existing workers would be displaced in the increased competition for jobs. We might add that productivity would also almost certainly decline as women pining to be hairdressers and beauticians were drafted into mixing concrete and driving trucks. We would, in fact, all end up worse off in terms of overall wellbeing (what economists refer to as 'welfare') because so many of us would now be engaged in activities which we did not want to do.[9]

The cost of employing thousands of people in the new equalities industry is real, and it bears down on company profits and taxpayers. But the supposed benefits, in terms of 'savings' generated by greater equality, exist mainly in the imaginations of those who produce these estimates. And many of them, of course, are themselves employed in the industry.

The EHRC: the heart of the Empire

At the centre of the equalities industry sits the Equality and Human Rights Commission, which was established in 2006 and employs more than 500 full-time staff. In 2009, it enjoyed a total budget of £63 million, of which £24 million went on wages. The Chair of the Commission got a salary of £112,000 (plus car and chauffeur), the part-time Commissioners shared another £317,000 between them, and the Chief Executive received £185,000 (substantially more than the Prime Minister).[10] The Commission's role, it should be remembered, is to promote equality.

After its first two years of operation, the EHRC issued a pamphlet summarising its achievements to date.[11] These included: fifty thousand queries answered by its helpline, £10 million of public money handed out in grants to 285 different groups, unsolicited advice sent to 136,000 businesses on managing their equality obligations during the economic downturn, three inquiries undertaken into employment discrimination, 70 research reports published, three thousand individuals and organisations consulted in a Human Rights Inquiry, and 80 discrimination cases provided with legal assistance. The EHRC has evidently been very busy, talking, advising and pushing out bits of paper. Whether all this activity has achieved anything worthwhile is largely a matter of opinion. Whether it has represented value for money can, however, be answered quite authoritatively.

In 2010, the House of Commons Public Accounts Committee published a damning report on the EHRC. It asked why it cost £39 million pounds to set up the organisation, given that it replaced three existing commissions regulating race, gender and disability discrimination. Over £9 million was blown buying new equipment and nobody at the EHRC could explain why it had not simply used the existing equipment bequeathed by its predecessors. Fourteen building leases were terminated, at a cost of almost £3 million, because the Commission wanted a new head office. Another £9 million went on salaries for the 83 members of the 'transition team,' who received average salaries of over £100,000 each over the 18 months when the Commission was being set up. £11 million went on an 'early exit' scheme, providing generous pay-offs to staff from the three predecessor commissions, some of whom were then immediately re-employed as consultants on generous commissions without any open competition for their posts.[12]

Even after it became fully operational, the EHRC continued to squander money. In 2007-08 it gave its staff an average pay rise of 6.8 per cent, in contravention of the remit agreed with the Treasury which specified a maximum of four per cent. In July 2009, it was employing a total of 574 full-time-equivalent staff, when only 525 had been authorised. In January 2010, it was paying its Interim Director General £1,000 per day while it dithered ineffectually to find a permanent replacement.[13] All this from an organisation which demands 'concerted action to decrease inequality, and increase fairness throughout our society'.[14]

In February 2011, the government announced that the EHRC budget is to be cut by almost 60 per cent in the course of this Parliament, from £60 to £22.5 million. This is expected to result in a halving of its workforce. According to a government spokesman, the Commission had 'not been careful enough with taxpayers' money'.[15] But as one hydra's head is lopped off, dozens more appear in its place.

Estimating the cost of equality monitoring in the public sector

The money squandered by the EHRC is just part of the overall government spend on equality and diversity monitoring, for every government department and public body of any size has for some years now been employing its own equality and diversity staff. There is no central register which might tell us how many people are employed altogether, nor what the cost is to the taxpayer of all this activity. But in research for this book, we have trawled web sites and annual reports, and we have contacted a small selection of public sector bodies, to try to get an impression of what has been going on across the board, in large organisations and in small.

We can begin with the Government Equalities Office, which was created in 2007 to oversee the EHRC. Its budget in 2009-10 amounted to £81 million. Although most of this (£62 million) went straight to the EHRC, there was still enough left to pay for 130 of its own staff (at a total cost of £6.5 million) and to fund about £10 million worth of 'projects', including £1.5 million spent on 'research'.[16]

Then there are the local Race Equality Councils and Equality Partnerships. Race Equality Councils were set up under the 1976 Race Relations Act to provide advice to victims of racial discrimination and to promote better race relations. They used to be funded by the Commission for Racial Equality (in conjunction with local authorities) before it was replaced by the EHRC, and in 2007-08, the CRE gave £4.24 million in grants to these councils. Its successor, the EHRC, still funds some of them (in 2009-10, it made grants worth £10 million to 61 different local organisations, including a handful of Racial Equality Councils), but most of its money now goes to other groups such as gypsy projects, women's centres, rape crisis centres, lesbian and gay support services, a women's prisoner support group, an ethnic alcohol counselling service, the National Youth Theatre and the Nottingham Playhouse Trust.

Racial Equality Councils nowadays rely mainly on local authorities and other public bodies for their money.[17] In recent years, they have evolved in many areas into broader 'equality partnerships' in which local councils are directly involved together with various voluntary groups. In these cases, the focus is on equality and diversity in general, not just on race, and council grants are an integral component of their income.[18]

Equality councils and partnerships can be found in most towns and counties in the UK. They are small organisations, each employing only a handful of people (a 2004 national audit found they employed an average of 8.25 staff, with numbers ranging from one to 25).[19] But there are a lot of them. Examples we looked at include:

- The Grampian Racial Equality Council, which is funded mainly by Aberdeen City Council (£97,000 in 2006-07), Aberdeenshire Council (£46,000), NHS Grampian (£14,000) and the Grampian Police (£25,000). Its total income in 2007-08 was £369,000.[20]

- Race Equality Action Lewisham, funded wholly by a grant from the London Borough of Lewisham which was worth £154,000 in 2008-09.[21]

- Plymouth and District Racial Equality Council, which employs ten members of staff and receives income in grants of £509,000 from a variety of public bodies including Plymouth City Council, Plymouth NHS, and various housing associations.[22]

- Peterborough Race Equality Council, which received £97,000 in grants in 2009-10, of which £54,000 came from the City Council, and £16,000 from the EHRC. It spent £72,000 on salaries.[23]

- Oxfordshire Racial Equality Council, which received £344,000 in 2008-09, of which £119,000 came from the EHRC, £31,000 from local district councils, and £8,000 from Thames Valley Police. It spent £305,000 on salaries.[24]

Assume one hundred such bodies, each employing eight staff (in line with the 2004 National Audit figures). This would imply a total employment figure of around 800, at an annual cost of around £25 million (meaning each council or partnership would be averaging an annual budget of around quarter of a million pounds, which looks about right judging by our mini-sample).

To get a more comprehensive view of the growth and scale of the equality and diversity industry, however, we need to look beyond these dedicated bodies, for most of the employment nowadays occurs elsewhere in the public sector, in central government departments, local authorities, police authorities, Primary Care Trusts and other quangos up and down the country. Most of these organisations have their own equality and diversity units, for they are required to monitor their staffing and their activities to demonstrate that they are in compliance with equalities legislation.[25]

For example, the Department of Environment, Food and Rural Affairs (DEFRA) is an average-sized government department in Whitehall. At the end of 2010, it was employing 2,570 core staff in its central London office (plus another 6,910 elsewhere).[26] It has its own diversity team in London which in 2009-10 employed 4.5 staff at a cost of £231,000. This team's work seems mainly to consist of researching the social make-up of DEFRA staff.[27] We can assume that other departments of a comparable size, like the Home Office, the Department of Health and the Department for Transport, employ similar diversity teams. Smaller departments, like Culture, Media and Sport, might get away with smaller units; larger ones, like Work and Pensions, might require larger ones. But in Whitehall alone, if DEFRA is any guide, we can estimate that at least one hundred equality and diversity staff are employed to monitor departmental staffing at an annual cost of around £5 million. Regional offices of central government will, of course, add substantially to this figure, as will the devolved Scottish, Welsh and Northern Ireland governments.

Local government, too, is an important employer in the equalities industry. We contacted several county councils, all of which had their own diversity teams which generally cost around £100 thousand each year to run.[28] A survey in 2010 by the Taxpayers Alliance found that local authorities were funding the equivalent of 543 full-time equivalent diversity posts in all, at a cost of almost £20 million.[29]

In research for this book, we also contacted a number of Primary Health Care Trusts and asked them for details of the money they spend on equality and diversity staffing and activities. We were told:

- Coventry employs three staff at a cost of £129,500 per year, plus £35,000 spent on an equality and diversity training programme for NHS employees—a total direct cost of £164,500.

- Worcester employs four full-time equivalent staff including a Team Administrator and two managers. It spends £240,000 on its Diversity Team, plus another £12,000 on training.

- Oxfordshire found it difficult to break down costs as 'promoting equality of access and outcomes should permeate through everything we do'. It claimed only one person was employed directly in equality and diversity at a cost of £41,000, with a further £6,500 spent on support software.

- Brighton and Hove employed only one full-time equality and diversity manager, but it estimated that it spent £88,300 on internal staffing and equality activities. It also contributes £1.14 million to external organisations such as local equality partnerships.

There are 152 PCTs in the country. If these four are in any way typical, we would estimate that they employ a total of between 300 and 500 people directly in promoting equality and diversity, and that they spend between £10 and £15 million on their own, in-house, activities. Grants and payments to outside organisations may add up to a lot more.

In 2007, it was announced that there were 1,162 quangos in the UK (although this figure included 469 local authorities) employing 714,000 staff and spending over £1bn.[30] It is impossible to say how many of these bodies employ equality and diversity staff, although most are required to monitor and report on the diversity of their staff as part of their public sector equality duty (we have seen that 27,000 public bodies in all are covered by the monitoring and reporting requirements of the 2010 Equality Act's 'equality duty'). The following may give some idea of the level of activity of the equalities industry across the various kinds of quangos:

- The Metropolitan Police claims to devote six per cent of its total annual budget (£187 million in 2006) to 'equalities related expenditure,' although some of this is accounted for by salaries for staff and officers working with minority communities. The Diversity and Citizen Focus Directorate employs 60 staff and costs the Met around £5 million per year to run.[31] All officers attend a mandatory two-day course on community and race relations, and in the first two weeks of service, officers spend four days attending a diversity course.[32] There are 43 other police authorities in England and Wales, although the Met is the largest.

- The Office for Fair Access is funded by the Department of Business Innovation and Skills to 'promote fair access to higher education,' and it spends its time monitoring the socio-economic profiles of students at universities. It has 4.5 members of staff, including a Director, and an expenditure of £546,000 in 2008-09.[33] Individual universities (of which there are well over one hundred) also employ their own diversity officers.

- After London won the bid for the 2012 Olympic Games, the Olympic Delivery Authority, responsible for developing the infrastructure for the Games, set up an Equality and Inclusion Team employing five senior-level managers on six-figure salaries to monitor diversity in companies bidding for construction and other contracts. It declined to divulge the total budget for this team.[34]

- The Equality and Diversity Forum is a charity funded in part by the European Community. It says the 'public benefit' derived from its work involves 'raising awareness in equality and diversity' and 'cultivating a sentiment in support of human rights and equality'. This costs £190,000 per annum, with staff costs of £89,000.[35]

The 2010 Equality Act will increase all this activity, for it imposed a new equality duty on 27,000 state bodies to audit the diversity of their staff each year. Those with 150 employees or more must also analyse patterns of service delivery to their client populations. The Government estimates that equality officers across the public sector will have to spend an extra eight days a year to generate these data, and that this will cost a total of £30 million every year (on top of existing equality and diversity budgets).[36] There will also be one-off costs in the first year, which are estimated at between £240.9m and £282.6m.[37]

Table 6.1: Estimated staff and budget figures for selected parts of the public sector equality and diversity industry

	Staff	Cost (£m)
EHRC	517	63.0
Equalities Office	130	19.0
Local equality councils	800	25.0
Whitehall departments	100	5.0
Local government	543	20.0
PCTs	400	13.0

This estimate allows us to make a rough overall estimate for the possible annual cost of equality and diversity monitoring in the public sector. If eight days of this work absorbs a total of £30 million of staffing costs, then in a full year, across the public sector as a whole, such work would cost the taxpayer around £600 million.[38] Grants, research and other associated activities will, of course, push this total even higher.

In March 2011, the Government Equalities Office announced some changes to the regulations specifying how the equality duty should be carried out. These changes were aimed at reducing costs by allowing organisations more scope to determine how they meet their equality duty. The new regulations place the onus on the organisations themselves to interpret their duty under the Act, leaving it to pressure groups and members of the public to hold them to account, rather than having to meet detailed outputs specified by Whitehall.[39] Whether this will actually reduce costs is, however, doubtful, for trades unions, user groups and political activists seem certain to push for as much information as they can get, and public bodies will still be under the same legal duties as they were before to provide it. The government itself admits that: 'The reshaped public sector Equality Duty will require public bodies to publish more information on equality than before,'[40] so it is unlikely that the regulatory cost will be trimmed much, if at all.

The cost of equalities legislation in the private sector

According to a 2009 survey by the Forum of Private Business, Britain's small and medium-size companies spend £2.4 billion every year complying with government employment legislation. This exceeds the amount they spend on complying with health and safety laws (£2.1 billion) and tax rules (£1.8 billion). Most of the cost is made up of time spent on paperwork, and £259 million of it comprises work associated with dismissals and redundancies. The survey attempted to isolate the specific cost of complying with equality and diversity legislation, and estimated this at £150 million for the service sector, £35 million for manufacturing, and £25 million for construction—a total of £210 million per annum across small and medium-size businesses as a whole.[41]

In the same year, the Institute of Directors, which represents larger companies, estimated that the new regulations contained in what became the 2010 Equality

Act (including the requirement to conduct gender pay audits) would cost its members another £71 million per year (this was on top of existing equality and diversity costs).[42] British Chambers of Commerce put the one-off cost to its members of implementing the Act at £189 million, with a net recurring additional annual cost thereafter of £3.5 million.[43]

The total cost of equalities monitoring in the private sector therefore probably amounts to between £300 and £400 million each year. Putting our estimates for the public and private sectors together, this gives a rough figure of £1 billion spent on staffing related to equality and diversity work, with other research and grants coming in on top of that.

The extension of equalities monitoring

The 2010 Equality Act allows the government to extend compulsory gender pay audits to the private sector in 2013. The Coalition government has made clear its support for the principle of gender pay audits in both the private and voluntary sectors (although it has dropped Labour's insistence that private companies which bid for public sector contracts should be required to publish their diversity statistics).[44] The intention is to leave it to companies themselves to introduce gender pay audits on a voluntary basis. Only if this fails to produce the results the government wants will the powers in the Equality Act be invoked to force companies to comply.[45]

The Coalition is also keen to press ahead with plans to push the private sector into appointing more women at senior management levels. When it came to power, the Coalition committed itself to promoting gender equality on company boards, and it appointed Lord Davies of

Abersoch to conduct a review.[46] He found that, in 2010, women accounted for only 13 per cent of FTSE 100 directors, eight per cent of FTSE 250 directors, and nine per cent of FTSE 350 directors. Their numbers were rising, but slowly (up from six per cent of FTSE 100 directors in 1999), and Davies argued for more radical change. He suggested this was 'as much about improving business performance as about promoting equal opportunities,' citing research apparently showing that companies with more women directors achieve a 42 per cent higher return on sales, a 53 per cent better return on equity, and are 20 per cent less likely to go bust.[47]

If these findings were as compelling as Davies suggests, of course, company shareholders would already be promoting more women onto boards, and there would be no need for government to intervene at all. As we have seen, it is a common ruse when new equalities regulation gets proposed for supporters to claim that it will save rather than cost money by increasing efficiency and raising output. Such evidence is rarely convincing, and in this particular case there is actually contrary evidence from a country that has gone down this road before us. Norway imposed legally-binding gender quotas on recruitment to company boards in the early years of this century, and research has found that the rapid increase in female participation which this triggered actually reduced profitability as companies struggled to find suitable women recruits.[48] Not surprisingly, the Davies Report fails to mention this research.

The Davies report stopped short of recommending Norwegian-style compulsory quotas, but it did suggest that FTSE 350 companies should all publish targets for increasing female representation on their boards, and that the target for the biggest one hundred companies should be a minimum of 25 per cent representation by 2015. In his Foreword to the report, Davies said the Government should 'introduce more prescriptive alternatives' if this voluntary system failed to deliver the intended results. The report further recommended that all quoted companies should every year be required to disclose their gender balance, not only on the board, but in senior executive positions and across the whole organisation, and that they should also all have 'boardroom diversity policies' linked to annual statements of progress made in achieving them. The Government welcomed the report, and Davies and his committee are now monitoring progress.

They may, however, be overtaken by events in Brussels. The EU wants all publicly-listed companies to have at least 40 per cent of their boards made up of women directors, and the Commission will soon bring forward a voluntary code to bring this about. If voluntarism fails, compulsion will follow.[49]

Tribunals

Employers do not only have to pay the costs of monitoring and reporting on the diversity of their staff and customer base. They also have to absorb the costs of discrimination and equal pay cases which are brought to employment tribunals, and the number of these cases has been rising fast in recent years.

The number of sex discrimination cases rose from 6,203 in 1998/9 to 28,153 in 2006/7, but has since fallen back to 18,637 in 2008/09—still a trebling in ten years. Equal pay cases mushroomed over the same period from 5,018 in 1998/9 to 45,748 ten years later, a staggering nine-fold increase. Other discrimination suits have been increasing as well: the number of race discrimination cases has almost doubled in ten years, to 4,983, and disability cases have risen 460 per cent, from 1,430 to 6,578, in the same period. The first age discrimination cases were brought in 2006/07, when just 942 cases were heard. Three years later, this had quadrupled to 3,801. The number of 'sexual orientation' and 'religion and belief' cases has also risen in the five years since these became actionable, from 349 to 600 in the case of the former, and from 307 to 832 in the case of the latter. In 2008-09, a total of 81,179 claims were adjudicated by employment tribunals, a five-fold increase in ten years.[50]

These figures represent clear evidence of the way equalities law seems to feed off itself. Not only has the number of victim categories kept expanding over the years, but the number of people claiming to be a victim within each of these categories has also grown, often quite dramatically. The result is almost an exponential rise in 'victimhood'. The emergence of 'no win-no fee' lawyers touting for business has undoubtedly facilitated this astonishing rate of increase, although new procedures for determining which jobs are equivalent to each other and should therefore be paid at the same rates probably contributed to the spike in sex discrimination and equal pay cases between 2006 and 2008. Most cases are brought against public sector employers, and many of the equal pay cases have been prompted by new Job Evaluation Schemes introduced in the NHS and local authorities.

It costs employers significant time and money every time an employee takes them to a tribunal (the average cost of an employment tribunal case to an employer is £5,393).[51] Research by the Chartered Institute of Personnel and Development found that the average time spent preparing a case was more than 16 days. And when a case is lost, there is also the cost of compensation: the average pay-out in 2006-07 was £15,059 in disability discrimination cases, £14,049 in race discrimination cases, and £10,052 in sex discrimination cases.[52]

Most cases that get to a tribunal, however, do not succeed. It costs a disgruntled employee or applicant nothing to air their grievance at a tribunal, and they stand to gain a tidy windfall if they succeed, so it is not surprising that many of the complaints that get brought turn out to be insubstantial.[53] Employers still have to incur costs in fighting such claims, however, and small companies on tight budgets often just pay up rather than contesting cases through to a tribunal. Three out of five claims are settled before the hearing, even though many are known to be trivial. The costs impact, not just on company profit sheets, but in a growing reluctance to take on new workers, for companies say that the problems they have in dismissing staff are a major factor deterring them from taking new people on in the first place.

In 2011, the Coalition Government promised to reform the system. One proposal is an extension of the qualifying period of employment before an unfair dismissal case can be brought, from one to two years, but this would have no effect on discrimination cases, where there is no minimum time requirement for employment (employers can even be sued by job applicants whom they have refused to employ). The Government is also considering a requirement that cases go to mediation before being brought before a tribunal, but an employer demand that plaintiffs be charged a fee (to deter frivolous claims) has been sent for further consultation.[54]

How big a bang for your buck?

It is very difficult to gauge the impact equalities legislation has had on the level of discrimination in British society, for we can never know what would have happened had all this intervention never occurred. Writing about America, Thomas Sowell notes how equalities researchers like to point to the growth of the black middle class after 1964 as evidence of the beneficial impact of the civil rights legislation of that year, yet the black middle class was growing faster before the Civil Rights Act was passed than after it.[55] Simple before-and-after comparisons can be very misleading, and it is difficult to gauge whether changes would have happened even without new laws.

Various UK studies have tried to assess the impact of our equalities laws by using modelling. Peter Dolton and his colleagues analyse the narrowing gender wage gap for graduates in the UK between the 1970s and 1990s and find that it had nothing to do with other changes going on in the labour market at that time (e.g. the imposition of incomes policies). They conclude the narrowing of the wage gap must have been due to the impact of sex equality laws, or to a convergence in male and female skill profiles.[56] Similarly, Wright and Ermisch claim that, while the gender pay gap persisted after the Sex Discrimination and Equal Pay Acts came into force, it did reduce, and this appears to reflect the impact of the legislation.[57] In a review of several studies, the Policy Studies Institute also estimates that the fall in the gender pay gap after 1975 was mainly due to a reduction in discrimination which it assumes can be explained by the legislation passed in that year.[58]

Targets and quotas clearly do have some effect (although we have seen that the UK has until now been rather ambivalent about imposing them). After setting a 40 per cent gender quota for company boards, for example, Norway raised the number of women company directors from seven per cent in 2002 to 44 per cent today (although we have seen that they seem to have paid a price in reduced efficiency and profitability, at least in the short-term). Spain introduced a similar law in 2007, giving companies until 2015 to comply, and female representation has so far risen from six per cent to 11 per cent. In Australia, where the Stock Exchange now requires companies to report on progress in expanding female board memberships, the number of new appointments going to women rose from five per cent to 27 per cent in just 12 months.[59]

But even if legislation such as the Equal Pay Act has had some effect in reducing inequalities, there has also been excess and indulgence which seems to have escalated as the laws have multiplied. Substantial sums of money have been squandered by government departments and agencies on courses, consultations and other activities of dubious value intended to meet their obligations under the 2010 Act.[60] The new equality duty on public sector agencies has spawned a number of initiatives which seem almost to have been designed as a slap in the face for taxpayers: a leadership course for gay, lesbian, bisexual and transsexual managers in the NHS; a 'Here Come The Girls' Home Office initiative to raise awareness of lesbian and bisexual staff; a consultation with more than 40 organisations by the Department for Transport to find whether protected groups are experiencing discrimination or harassment on board ships and hovercraft (they aren't).

The requirement to carry out impact assessments every time policy changes has also generated a lot of unnecessary and wasteful activity and expense. The Department for Environment, Food and Rural Affairs (Defra) paid £100,000 to consultants to investigate how boosting fish stocks in coastal waters might impact on protected groups including gays, Chinese and Welsh speakers. At the Department for Culture, Media and Sport, an equality impact assessment was needed to ensure minority groups participated fully in the Queen's Diamond Jubilee celebrations. And the Department of Energy and Climate Change had to work out if any protected groups had been unduly affected when it suspended its home insulation grants. It found that pregnant women, disabled people and elderly people might be adversely affected, but gays, transsexuals and singles/couples would be okay.

All of this has been going on while the Government struggles to contain the biggest blow-out of public sector debt since World War II.

7

Are Unequal Outcomes
Always Unfair?

Evidence of unequal outcomes

Under the terms of the 2006 Equality Act, the Equality and Human Rights Commission is required to report every three years on Britain's 'progress' towards becoming a more equal society. In 2010, the Commission published the first of these reports, entitled *How Fair Is Britain?*[1] It runs to 749 pages, and is packed with data focusing on statistical differences between the various 'protected groups' and the rest of the population. Although social class is not a legally-protected identity, the report also spends quite a lot of time on class differences too.

Descriptive statistics on each of the protected groups are presented for 40 different 'indicators' representing those aspects of people's lives which are thought to be crucial in enabling them to be 'happy, productive and fulfilled'.[2] These include life expectancy, homicide rates, imprisonment rates, vulnerability to crime, fear of crime, long-term illness, healthy lifestyles, child development, school and university performance, pay differentials, job 'segregation', poverty rates, housing conditions, access to child care, involvement in offering unpaid care, and representation in elected bodies.

On many of these indicators, the report finds significant differences of outcomes between members of different groups.[3] People in higher socio-economic groups live on average seven years longer than those in the lowest social classes. Black Caribbean and Pakistani babies suffer twice the infant mortality rates of white and Bangladeshi babies. Black people are more likely to be murdered (and are more likely to die at the hands of the police) than white people. Gays and lesbians attempt suicide more often than heterosexuals. Ethnic minorities are more likely to be stopped and searched by the police, and blacks are five times more likely to be imprisoned than whites. Christians are ten times less likely to report harassment than members of other faiths, and two-thirds of gays and lesbians have experienced a homophobic crime or incident in the last three years. Pakistani and Bangladeshi people are twice as likely as whites to report they are in poor health, and they also have higher rates of mental illness. People in lower social classes smoke more and exercise less than those in higher social classes. Children from poorer homes (defined as those who are eligible for free school meals) score less well on child development measures, are more than twice as likely to end up permanently excluded from school, and do half as well at GCSE exams as other children. Black Caribbean people (even those for whom English is a first language) have lower levels of functional literacy than whites, and Bangladeshis and Pakistanis are less well-qualified and are less likely to be employed. People over 50 find it harder to get a job than younger applicants. Less than half of disabled people are 'economically active', compared with almost 80 per cent of non-disabled people. Women, disabled people, south Asians and Muslims all have lower average pay than white Christian men, and women are less likely than men to reach higher level positions at work. Twice as many Pakistani and Bangladeshi families with children suffer material deprivation as white families. Single mothers and ethnic minorities are more likely to be living in sub-standard or overcrowded housing. Women and ethnic minorities are under-represented in local and national assemblies.

The report is not all negative. It commends us for the 'progress' we have made in recent years in tolerating diversity and endorsing equality. It regrets that many of us are still 'uneasy' about mass immigration, and that we are 'suspicious' and 'disapproving' of gypsies and travellers, but it puts these attitudes down to our exposure to the media.[4] It notes with approval that few of us any longer believe in traditional gender roles;[5] it seems pleased that only a quarter of the workforce still conforms to 'the old standard model of being white, male, non-disabled and under the age of 45';[6] and it congratulates us on moving in less than 20 years from 'vilifying same-sex relationships' (it means the legislation outlawing the promotion of homosexuality in schools) to legally recognising them (through civil partnerships).[7] It claims that an egalitarian agenda now commands widespread political support in Britain,[8] and it detects in the population as a whole a 'shared aspiration towards greater equality'.[9]

Nevertheless, the conclusion it draws from the evidence on the persistence of unequal outcomes is that Britain is still a very unfair place to live. In his Foreword to the report, Trevor Phillips writes: 'All too many of us remain trapped by the accident of our births, our destinies far too likely to be determined by our sex or race... We are not as yet a fair society.'[10] While giving us a tick for the 'progress' we have made, the report therefore concludes that we still have a long way to go: 'Outcomes for many people are not shifting as far or as fast as they should.' It also predicts that 'new forms of inequality' are likely to become entrenched 'without some form of corrective action'.[11] Notwithstanding the avalanche of legislation in this area in recent years, it seems that even more intervention is now required if we are to sort this problem out.

Unequal outcomes and fairness

In his review of the development of affirmative action around the world, Thomas Sowell notes that social groups rarely, if ever, perform exactly the same as each other on any social indicator. Moreover, the differences between them tend to persist over time and across countries and regions, even when governments do their best to eradicate them. This persistence fuels ever-more intense efforts by politicians to overcome group differences by adopting affirmative action strategies designed to smooth the path of those they see as disadvantaged. The more these efforts fail, as they generally do, the more effort gets devoted to reinforcing them.[12]

The history of equalities legislation in Britain since the 1960s perfectly illustrates Sowell's argument. We have seen that legislation has been progressively strengthened as time has gone on, yet in 2010, the EHRC was still able to produce a weighty report documenting hundreds of examples of one group out-performing or under-performing another. Predictably, the solution that is put forward is more intervention, more 'corrective action'. In the equalities business, nothing succeeds like failure.

The EHRC's belief that Britain is still a fundamentally unfair society rests on the assumption that different outcomes between different social groups reflect the unequal conditions and opportunities under which they operate. We have seen that this is an assumption which this report shares with most of the other research that gets published in this area (including, as we saw in chapter 5, the wretched Macpherson Report). But it is flawed. What the EHRC fails to acknowledge is that average differences in group outcomes commonly arise for all sorts of reasons. Lack of social opportunity is only one possible cause among many.

The report finds, for example, that children from lower social classes get fewer good GCSEs than middle-class children, but it never asks whether this might reflect lower average ability levels, rather than (or as well as) because they are poor.[13] It complains that lower-class adults die younger than those in the middle class, but it swiftly passes over the fact that they also smoke more and exercise less.[14] The fact that more Pakistani babies die in infancy than white babies is unlikely to reflect their poor social conditions, given that Bangladeshi babies enjoy a better infant mortality rate than white babies even though their families tend to be more deprived. But the report never stops to consider this oddity, preferring to stick with the comfortable assumption that inequality is somehow or other to blame (we shall see in chapter 9 that the actual explanation is probably that Pakistani infants suffer disproportionately from congenital defects brought about by high rates of cousin inter-marriage).

The same kinds of objections can be applied right across the board. The reason many Pakistani and Bangladeshi women stay out of the workforce probably has little or nothing to do with exclusion by racist or misogynist employers, but reflects a cultural emphasis on a more traditional gender division of labour. The fact that women tend on average to earn less than men does not necessarily mean they are unfairly paid; it may simply reflect the fact that many of them prefer to take career breaks when their children are young, and this disrupts their earnings progression. If more black kids are stopped by the police, this does not automatically mean the cops are racist; perhaps black youngsters are simply out on the streets in greater numbers than whites.

We shall see in chapters 8 and 9 that, in many cases, these alternative explanations stand up a lot better than the EHRC's assumption that discrimination is always to blame. The EHRC and other equalities campaigners too swiftly assume that the test of fairness lies simply in an analysis of outcomes. But before leaping to the conclusion that inequality signifies discrimination, we need first to investigate the processes that generate these outcomes. In his Foreword, the EHRC chairman blames a 'web of prejudice' for the results his report contains. But he offers little or no evidence that such a web exists. He simply imputes its existence from the evidence on differential outcomes. This is an extremely dangerous thing to do. We might even complain that it is unfair.

The fallacy of proportionate outcomes

The core assumption that underpins the EHRC's recent report, and which characterises a lot of other equalities research and monitoring, is that individual qualities and preferences are equally distributed across all groups in the population. This is what Thomas Sowell calls the 'assumption about numbers', and it is nearly always false.

If blacks were the same as whites in all respects, if women were the same as men, if disabled people were the same as able-bodied people, and if old people were the same as young, then we would not expect to find any significant differences between any of these groups as regards their average employment levels, pay rates, health indicators, imprisonment rates, educational achievements or other socio-economic outcomes. If we did find significant differences between them—that men earn significantly more than women, for example, or that blacks leave school with significantly fewer qualifications than whites—then we might be justified in assuming that something must have happened to one group, but not to the other, which generated the unequal outcomes between them. We would be justified, in other words, in positing the existence of some sort of discrimination or unfair practice as a reasonable explanation for the differences.

This is essentially the logic that the equalities industry follows. It starts out from the assumption that there should be no differences between groups in their performance on various key indicators, and when it finds a difference (as invariably it does), it attributes it to the existence of discrimination of one form or another. But this is only reasonable if these groups are all the same in terms of their members' individual attributes, actions, beliefs and capacities. If they are not the same, then different outcomes may well reflect individual variations and have nothing whatever to do with unfair treatment by others.

There are basically two ways of explaining unequal group outcomes, but equalities campaigners are only ever interested in exploring one of them. The kind of explanation they favour points to exogenous, or *contextual* factors which impact differently on different groups. Thus, there are more black people in prison because the police are more likely to arrest black than white suspects; there are more kids from private schools at Oxbridge because admission tutors fail to recognise the potential of applicants from inner city comprehensives; there are more men than women company directors because women's career progress is thwarted by having to care for young children; and so on.

The other type of explanation, which is generally ignored or downplayed by equalities campaigners, points to the importance of endogenous, or *compositional* factors in generating different average outcomes between groups. Groups differ because they are composed of individuals with different characteristics and attributes.[15] Seen in this way, higher black imprisonment rates reflect the fact that black youths commit more crime; the success of private school pupils in getting into Oxbridge reflects the higher average intelligence and motivation levels of children born to successful parents; and the small number of women in the board room comes about because women on average have different aspirations and career preferences than men.

We cannot say in advance whether contextual or compositional factors are the principal explanation for any particular incidence of group differences. But any attempt to explain unequal group outcomes with reference to contextual factors should obviously first ensure that compositional factors are not to blame. Explanation of group differences, in other words, should begin by investigating the possible contribution made by individual elements before rushing to attribute causal responsibility to wider contextual factors. Or to put it more simply: we should always check the extent to which individuals are the source of their own disadvantage before deciding that they are the victims of group circumstances beyond their control.

This is not, however, the procedure generally favoured by equalities campaigners. Faced with evidence of group differences, they assume from the outset that contextual factors are to blame.[16] Compositional factors are an unattractive place for them to start looking for explanations because there is not much government can do to change them. If groups vary because of the characteristics of their individual members, we would have to engineer a change in the attributes or behaviour of a large proportion of these individuals in order to bring about greater equality. If working-class children do worse in school because on average they do not work as hard as their middle-class contemporaries, or if men outnumber women in senior managerial positions because many women prefer to devote more of their time and effort to raising their children, or if young black males are over-represented in jails because they commit a dispro-portionate amount of the crime, then the different average outcomes of these groups will never disappear until large numbers of working-class children, women or black adolescents can be convinced to change the way they think or behave. This could take a long time, the results are uncertain, and there are uncomfortable political problems of moral relativism that have to be negotiated along the way (not least, what is to be done if people do not want to change in the direction required by the intervention).

Contextual or exogenous factors therefore represent a much more attractive place for egalitarians to start looking for explanations. Explanations pointing to contextual factors avoid having to attribute responsibility for disadvantageous outcomes to those who suffer them by locating the causes of 'social disadvantage' outside of the groups which experience it. There is therefore no danger of 'blaming the victim', nor any need to try to change people's behaviour—all you have to do is 'reform the system'.

Contextual explanations see unequal group outcomes as the product of the different conditions within which groups operate. These differences may take the form of conscious, discriminatory actions by people in other groups (e.g. class snobbery excluding lower-class applicants from prestigious universities, or racial discrimination preventing ethnic minority candidates from rising to top positions in management hierarchies). But as we saw in chapter 4, they may also reflect the operation of 'institutional bias', or what sociologists have called 'structures of domination'.[17] In this latter case there may be no evidence at all of an intent or motivation by others to bring about patterns of disadvantage. It just happens because of the way procedures are set up. Examples include the existence of a patriarchal 'glass ceiling,' which is blamed for hindering women's career advancement, and the existence of 'institutional racism,' which has been blamed for generating and reproducing social disadvantages for various ethnic minority groups.

As we saw in chapter 4, the beauty of explanations like these is that they are effectively immune to falsification. It makes no difference if individual men are found not to be sexist, or if individual whites are found not to hold racist views, for the problem is patriarchy, not male individuals; racism, not individual white people. Indeed, if male or white individuals appeal to their own non-sexist or non-racist values and beliefs as counter-evidence, this can be taken as confirming evidence that the problem exists, for it indicates their failure to understand and acknowledge their roles as the unwitting agents of sexist and racist systems.

Because these 'system properties' cannot be directly observed, they have to be 'measured' through indirect indicators. And the only indicators to hand are the statistics pointing to different group outcomes. At this point, the whole argument becomes beautifully circular and self-confirming. The indirect empirical 'indicators' which 'prove' the existence of patriarchy, institutional racism, ageism or whatever turn out to be indistinguishable from the empirical outcomes that the research set out to explain in the first place. Unequal outcomes are thus explained as the product of systemic factors whose operation can only be detected in the existence of unequal outcomes! It is the perfect Catch 22. The claim of unfairness becomes immune to any possible falsification.

8

Unequal Labour
Market Outcomes

There is no doubt that sometimes individuals get unfairly treated in the labour market as a result of their race, sex or some other characteristic. There is clear evidence, for example, that employers discriminate against applicants who appear to be from ethnic minorities, even when they know nothing else about them. This has been demonstrated by sending batches of fictitious but comparable applications to employers who are advertising vacancies. Applications made using ethnic minority names do less well in securing interviews, and this has been true throughout the period when race discrimination in employment has been unlawful.

In one study of accounting and financial services in the 1970s, 85 per cent of apparently British applicants got through the initial screening stage, compared with 53 per cent of Africans, 48 per cent of West Indians, and 44 per cent of Indians or Pakistanis.[1] In the 1990s, researchers found that people with non-European surnames were less likely to be admitted to medical schools, even when their qualifications were comparable to those of other candidates.[2] And most recently, in 2009, the Department of Work and Pensions sent off almost three thousand applications for jobs across Britain in IT, accountancy, sales, HR, teaching and care assistants and general office work, using names commonly associated with different ethnic identities, and found that 10.7 per cent of those with a British name received a positive response, compared with 6.2 per cent of those with an ethnic minority name. Discrimination was most pronounced in smaller, private sector employers.[3]

Less compelling evidence of discrimination can be gleaned from surveys which have asked members of protected groups if they have experienced it. Unsurprisingly, perhaps, many report that they have. Almost six out of ten workers say their careers have been affected by age discrimination,[4] although only three per cent say they have been rejected for a job because of their age.[5] Ageism allows even well-heeled middle-class professionals to join the ranks of the victims (one-third of college lecturers think they have been victims of age discrimination, for example).[6]

Claims that racism, sexism and disabilism have blighted career progress are also common. Just one per cent of whites, but seven per cent of ethnic minority people, believe they have been rejected for a job because of their race,[7] and four in ten ethnic minority nurses say they have been harassed by work colleagues on account of their race.[8] Half of working women say they have been sexually harassed.[9] Nearly a quarter of disabled people say they have been discriminated against in the last year while trying to access goods and services.[10] How many of these claims are true, and how serious these incidents were, no-one knows.

Most of the research claiming to find discrimination in employment is not based on experiments or surveys, however. It is based on the statistical observation that 'victim groups' appear to be performing worse on pay, employment levels, promotion, or some other relevant measure, than other people are. The existence of these average group differences is then taken as evidence that they are subject to unequal conditions and opportunities.

Many researchers have, for example, reported that ethnic minorities fare worse in the competition for jobs than whites. They have higher unemployment rates, even after controlling for differences in their work experience levels and qualifications.[11] Black rates of entry into higher-level jobs are also about ten percentage points below what they 'should' be given their average qualifications and work experience.[12] When researchers find differences like these, they commonly explain them as the result of discrimination in the labour market. If the qualifications are the same, and the work experience is the same, then the assumption is that different outcomes *must* be due to unfair selection and promotion procedures.

But as we saw in the previous chapter, this is not *necessarily* the explanation for such differences. There are many possible reasons why one ethnic group might perform better than another in the competition for jobs, and few of them get measured by the variables included in economists' models. Researchers try to control for differences in levels of qualifications and work experience, but a lot of other individual differences between group memberships are ignored. The 'unexplained residuals' which researchers come up with might indicate the effect of discrimination, but they might also be caused by factors they haven't measured and cannot measure, including differences in average motivation levels, reliability, social skills or even the reluctance of some ethnic groups to participate in mainstream society.[13]

To explore these issues further, we shall focus on the question of gender discrimination, where a huge amount of research has now been done into why women seem to be promoted into senior positions at a lower rate than men, and why women's pay continues to lag behind that of men.

A glass ceiling?

Ever since 1975, it has been illegal for employers to appoint or promote people on the basis of their gender. However, despite this, research continues to find that women are under-represented in senior positions across many occupations. In 2002, for example, women made up 35 per cent of hospital consultants, 24 per cent of law partners, 21 per cent of senior civil servants and just six per cent of company directors. Statistics like these are used to support the argument that women encounter a *'glass ceiling'* — an 'invisible, implicit but impenetrable barrier which prevents women from reaching senior positions within organisations' — in many professions.[14] They are blocked partly because they have to take on child-care responsibilities at a crucial point in their career development, and partly because they get shut out of influential, informal, male-dominated social networks.[15] They are therefore directly and indirectly discriminated against.

One of the problems in evaluating evidence like this is that it can take many years for people to reach the top jobs. This means that if traditional barriers to women do get removed, we are unlikely to see the results until some decades later. Research on recruitment of hospital consultants, for example, has found that, while there are fewer female than male consultants, the 'glass ceiling' has almost certainly disappeared in most areas of medicine, for the promotion profiles of younger entrants now look much the same for both sexes. Women doctors are now coming through to the top positions in proportion to their numbers entering medical school 30 years earlier.[16] Similarly, there is evidence that women in business are now reaching senior management positions in greater numbers, and that they may even be progressing up career ladders faster than their male counterparts.[17]

Few equalities advocates are impressed by findings like these, however.[18] Accepting that the proportion of female company directors has increased (by almost 50 per cent in seven years, from nine per cent to 13 per cent), Lord Davies's recent investigation nevertheless complained that progress in the corporate sector is 'not good enough'. At the current rate, says his report, it would take 'decades' for 'significant' changes to work through 'without other interventions'.[19] Other researchers claim that, even when women have succeeded in breaking through at lower levels, new glass ceilings get reinstated a bit higher up to block them again.[20] Almost everyone seems to agree that new policies are needed to force organisations to accept more women at the top.

The gender pay gap

The problem is not limited to promotions into top jobs. Women also seem to be paid less than men on average.

For more than 40 years, researchers have been reporting the existence of a so-called 'gender pay gap'.[21] Figures for April 2010 show that median full-time hourly pay was £13.01 for men and £11.68 for women—a 'pay gap' of 10.2 per cent.[22] According to the EHRC, this difference in average pay rates has been 'stubbornly persistent', and it suggests (wrongly, as it turns out) that, while the gap has narrowed over the last 30 years, 'progress' now 'seems to have stalled'.[23]

Equalities campaigners and left-wing politicians are understandably agitated about the persistence of this gender pay gap, and taken together with concerns about the 'glass ceiling' on promotions, it fuels their determination to keep tightening equalities law. The Fawcett Society, which campaigns on women's issues, says 'women who work full-time are being ripped off by £4,000 a year due to the pay gap'.[24] The EHRC's National Director in Scotland, Rose Micklem, says: 'There is plenty of evidence that the gender equality revolution is "unfinished". The most recent figures for the pay gap between women and men in full-time work [are] shocking.'[25]

But are women really being 'ripped off'? Are these statistics so shocking? To make sense of evidence about 'glass ceilings' and 'gender pay gaps', we obviously have to ask what is producing these differences. In particular, we need to know whether women are trying for the same occupations as men in the same numbers, and once in a job, whether they are equally ambitious for advancement. On both counts, interesting gender differences emerge, and when we take account of these, much of the difference between male and female rates of progress and levels of remuneration can be explained.

Do women have the same preferences as men?

Women tend to cluster in different kinds of occupations from men. They take up more than nine in ten apprenticeships in childcare, business administration and hairdressing, for example, but fewer than one in 30 in construction and engineering.[26] Women gravitate towards courses in medicine (80 per cent female), veterinary science (76 per cent), education (76 per cent) and languages (68 per cent), but men are concentrated in courses in engineering and technology (84 per cent), computer science (81 per cent) and architecture, building and planning (69 per cent).[27] While 83 per cent of personal service workers and 77 per cent of secretarial and administrative workers are female, 94 per cent of engineers and 86 per cent of architects, planners and surveyors are male.[28] Women also cluster in public sector employment in far greater numbers (40 per cent compared with only 15 per cent of men).

These marked differences obviously reflect the fact that men and women often have different interests and are drawn to different kinds of careers, but they are seen as a problem by equalities campaigners. The EHRC, for example, thinks there should be no occupational differences between men and women, and it explains the differences that do exist as the product of stereotyping and conditioning ('cultural expectations'): 'There is no inherent reason why today's instances of educational segregation should persist: but the fact that they have remained, while others have diminished rapidly or disappeared altogether, suggests that they may be unlikely to change today without some form of intervention.'[29] Put simply: even the brightest and best-educated women don't know what's good for them, so the Commission must step in to stop so many of them becoming vets, and force them into becoming engineers instead.[30]

There is little room in this kind of thinking for individual volition as a causal explanation for inter-group differences. The EHRC never asks whether women might select caring careers because they are, on average, better at nurturing, and therefore get more satisfaction from caring professions than men do, or that men are drawn to engineering because on average, they perform better on spatial tasks and therefore enjoy them more. Such propositions are ruled out in advance as 'ideological,' even though there is substantial evidence for them.[31] Instead, preferences are assumed to reflect social pressure and conditioning, not free and informed choice.[32]

It's the same story when it comes to the choices people make once they have begun their careers. One reason there are relatively few female company directors, for example, is that many women take time out from careers when they start a family. The Davies report on women company directors found that male and female graduates enter companies in similar numbers, and this proport-ionality is maintained as they move into junior management positions. But women start to fall behind at higher levels as they take time out to raise families, leaving the men to press ahead in their careers.

Career breaks to raise children are also the key explanation for the gender pay gap. Most women take a substantial break from work once they start a family. Half the mothers of three-year-olds are not working at all, and most of the rest are only working part-time.[33] It is these career breaks that produce lower median pay rates after the age of 30.

Even the EHRC accepts that pay differences are small or non-existent when men and women are in their twenties, before most of them have children. Indeed, in the 22 to 29 age group, the gender pay gap is actually reversed—full-time women workers earn 2.1 per cent *more* on average than full-time male workers in this age group.[34] It is only later that the gap switches to favour men, and then starts to widen.[35] The reason is family commitments. Women who do not have a career break enjoy much better earnings than those who do.[36] Indeed, women who do not settle down with a partner and have children more than keep pace with men in their earnings throughout their careers—men who are not married or cohabiting actually earn 1.1 per cent *less* on average than women who are not married or cohabiting.[37] The reason women earn less than men on average is simply that many more of them choose to divide their time between work and family.

Is it unfair that women's pay and career development often suffer when they have children? It all depends on whether their decision to refocus towards child rearing and away from career development is coerced or voluntary. The equalities industry seems in no doubt that women are coerced by lack of choice, and the recent Davies report also buys into this assumption. It says women drop-out at higher levels of management because of a 'lack of flexible working arrangements' and 'difficulties in achieving a work-life balance'.[38] Other, shriller voices talk darkly of 'male-dominated power structures' which seek to exclude successful career women and force them into 'abandoning their jobs'.[39]

But the evidence suggests that many women *prefer* a different balance between work and family commitments compared with men. Recent research by the Institute of Leadership and Management found that women managers tend to be less single-minded when it comes to career ambitions than men are. Many want to divide their focus between work and family responsibilities.[40] And in path-breaking research, Catherine Hakim has shown that about 20 per cent of UK women are strongly home-centred, 20 per cent are clearly career-centred, but the rest seek to combine the two, and are happy to make such compromises as are appropriate in each area of their lives. In short, few women are forced to sacrifice their careers for their families. Most exercise a clear preference about the weight they wish to place on each aspect of their lives.[41]

The equalities industry places great emphasis on provision of childcare facilities so that more women can keep working when they start families, but the evidence is that most women prefer to reduce the time they spend at work so they can spend more time with their children. Nearly two-thirds of working mothers of pre-school or school-age children would prefer to reduce their current working hours, even if better child care were available, and lack of suitable child care is rarely the reason women give for stopping working when they have children.[42] A 2009 YouGov poll found that only 12 per cent of mothers wanted to work full-time and 31 per cent did not want to work at all. Just one per cent of mothers with children under five thought women in their situation should work full-time, and 49 per cent thought they should not work at all, provided their partners were working.[43]

The equalities industry thinks sex roles should be symmetrical—i.e. men and women should divide their time between work and home in exactly the same way.[44] But research on women's preferences shows that about 80 per cent of them do not want to focus single-mindedly on careers, in the way that many men do. What the equalities industry thinks women should want does not therefore reflect what most women actually want. This is confirmed by experience in Norway, where mothers have been given the choice between free child care (so they can continue working) and cash payments in lieu of a childcare place (so they can raise their children at home). Four times as many choose the latter option.[45] Most working mothers are not pushed out of the labour force; they jump.

Modelling gender differences in labour market outcomes

So why does the idea persist that women are being unfairly treated? Economists and their models are mainly to blame. Using multivariate modelling techniques, economists have tried to pin down how much of the gender pay gap can be explained by differences in the qualifications and experience that men and women bring to their jobs. Any gap in earnings which remains unexplained once 'relevant' variables have been taken into account is then put down to sex discrimination. And invariably, there is always a residual.[46]

An obvious problem with these studies is that not everything is, or can be, measured. Almost every research paper finds that some gap in earnings still remains, even after taking account of differences such as higher male qualifications, greater male work experience or career breaks by women raising children. But to then assume that this remaining residual must be due to sex discrimination is clearly illegitimate.[47] There is an infinity of factors not included in these models, and the unexplained portion of the wage gap could be due to any number of them. Sex discrimination is certainly one possibility, but there are many other candidates as well.

One is that men tend to work in less desirable jobs which have to pay more to attract recruits. They are more likely to work outside in all weathers, to work unsocial hours, to travel further to work, to receive less training, to be vulnerable to redundancy, to take time off work and to report low levels of job satisfaction.[48] Employers only pay what they have to in order to fill their vacancies, so if on average, men earn more than women with similar levels of skill and experience, it is probably because they are doing jobs which require a higher wage for the market to clear. Even when men and women have similar levels of qualifications (e.g. as graduates), they tend to specialise in different kinds of skills (e.g. men do science degrees in much larger numbers), and these often command different levels of remuneration in the labour market.

As we have seen, men also often differ from women in their preferences as between work and family commitments. Economists' models have become more sophisticated over time, and some attempt has been made in more recent work to build preferences into the analysis, but the measurement of preferences is still only indirect, and leaves much to be desired. In a paper for the Policy Studies Institute, for example, Steve Lissenburgh estimates that about two-fifths of the gender pay gap is down to differences between men's and women's qualifications and experience, a quarter of it reflects the greater time women take out from work for child rearing, and about one-third of it is due to 'discrimination'.[49] He estimates the size of the 'discrimination' factor by measuring the different returns to men and women with similar levels of full-time work experience, the assumption being that 'men's and women's motivations for undertaking full-time employment are very similar'.[50] But is this a legitimate assumption to make?

The results of research on a sample of 10,000 UK students who graduated in 1995 suggests it may not be. Arnaud Chevalier found a gender pay gap 42 months after graduation of 12.6 per cent.[51] Using standard decomposition methods, he was able to account for almost all (84 per cent) of it without resorting to catch-all discrimination explanations.

Chevalier showed that, partly, the pay gap arises because men choose to study subjects which offer higher financial returns (science majors, for example, can expect to earn more than those in the humanities and social sciences). Partly, it reflects women's preference for public sector employment, which has historically tended to offer lower wages in return for greater security, flexibility and pension rights. Partly, it is because women look for different things in a career. They value 'social usefulness' and job satisfaction much more than men do; men, on the other hand, put a lot more weight on financial rewards and the prospects for career development, and are much more likely to describe themselves as ambitious. And crucially, Chevalier also showed that women's choices often reflect their anticipation of a future career break to have children; in other words, they select less intense jobs even before starting a family, because these will allow them to find the balance they want between home and career.

Chevalier concluded that a large portion of the gender pay gap reflects the different choices that men and women make about their desired careers. 'Discrimination', he says' 'is limited.'[52] But most research and writing by the equalities industry ignores findings like this. Failing to take account of differences in what men and women commonly look for in their jobs, it is happy to conclude that discrimination 'must' be the explanation for the differences it finds. More heavy-handed government intervention is then proposed in order to put the situation right.

Labour market 'discrimination' on grounds of disability, ethnicity and sexual orientation

As with women, so too with other protected groups, different labour market outcomes, such as different average rates of pay or different levels of employment, are too readily explained by equalities researchers as the product of discrimination, even when other explanations remain unexplored.

Research on disabled people, for example, commonly reports a 'disability pay gap' of eight or nine per cent. After analysing the impact of personal characteristics like qualifications and experience, about half of this difference remains unexplained, and this residual is then attributed to 'discrimination'.[53] But there are crucial 'productivity differences' between disabled and able-bodied workers which are likely to impact on their levels of employment and rates of pay. Once these are taken into account, the apparent 'discrimination' against disabled workers completely disappears.[54]

Many researchers have also reported that ethnic minorities have lower employment rates than whites, even after controlling for differences in work experience and qualification levels.[55] Again, this difference is assumed to indicate discrimination in the labour market.[56] But there are many other possible explanations which are rarely examined in these models. Why attribute the unexplained residual to discrimination rather than, say, differences in attitudes? We saw earlier that there is evidence that some ethnic minority workers do not even want to participate in the mainstream economy.[57] Shouldn't we therefore at least check whether blacks, whites and Asians are all equally determined to find work, and are equally committed to working hard in their jobs when they do get employment, rather than leaping straight away to the conclusion that ethnic minorities are being excluded from jobs illegitimately?

And then there is the question of the 'gay pay gap'. You may not have heard of this, because it never gets discussed, but gay men and lesbians tend to earn *more* than heterosexual men and women.[58] Gay men also tend to cluster in particular kinds of occupations, just as women do, but in the case of gays, this clustering is never seen as a 'problem' by equalities campaigners. As we shall see in the next chapter, differential outcomes are seen as clear evidence of 'discrimination' by the equalities industry only when they point in the expected direction. When protected groups do better than other people, which they quite often do, such differences simply get ignored.

9

Inequalities in Social Outcomes

The various 'protected groups' do not only vary from the norm when it comes to employment outcomes. They vary statistically on many other social indicators as well, including educational achievement, social mobility rates, health and morbidity and crime. Wherever they are found to be lagging behind the norm, discrimination or 'systemic bias' tends to get blamed, even though other factors are generally at work. Sometimes, however, they exceed the norm, and when this happens, everyone in the equalities industry tends to fall silent.

Family support: black underachievement in school

In the late 1970s, the UK government became increasingly concerned about the 'underachievement' of black school-children relative to whites. It set up a committee of inquiry under Anthony Rampton, and its first report, *West Indian Children In Our Schools*, was published in 1981. It laid the blame firmly on racism, negative and hostile teachers and a biased curriculum. The final report, *Education for All*, published under Lord Swann's chairmanship in 1985, identified a wider range of explanatory factors, but it still argued that the answer lay in the development of a 'multicultural education' more relevant to black children's lives.[1]

Since the 1980s, the under-performance of black children compared with whites has narrowed (in a period when examinations have been dumbed down and pass rates have increased every year, a narrowing was almost

121

inevitable, for it has become increasingly difficult *not* to pass GCSEs).[2] But despite this, the template laid down by Rampton's report continues to influence public debate, and politicians and academics can still be found attacking our schooling system as 'racist', criticising teachers for 'failing' black children, and arguing that schooling must be made more 'relevant' to black students if they are to overcome the multiple obstacles they face.[3]

What has been conspicuously missing through much of this debate on why black children underachieve, however, is the obvious complementary question of why children from some other ethnic minority groups 'overachieve' relative to whites. If the problem is a racist school system, bigoted teachers or a slanted curriculum, how is it that Indian children going through the British school system seem not only to do better than black Caribbean children, but better also than white children?

The EHRC's *How Fair Is Britain?* report tells us that as early as age five, Indian children have developed cognitive skills as fully as white British children, but both groups are well ahead of black and Pakistani children.[4] Once they get to school, children from Asian families are less likely to be excluded for bad behaviour than children from white or black Caribbean families,[5] and by the time they take GCSEs, Indian and Chinese pupils comfortably out-perform everybody else. The proportion of students achieving five or more good GCSE passes including maths and English are: Chinese 72 per cent; Indian 67 per cent; Bangladeshi, white British and black African 51 per cent; Pakistani 43 per cent; and black Caribbean 39 per cent.[6]

Similar patterns arise in further and higher education. About 23 per cent of university admissions in Britain go to ethnic minority candidates, and this is roughly what would be expected given their representation in the younger age groups in this country. But Indians and Chinese are 'over-represented' among graduates, while black Caribbeans and Pakistanis are once again bringing up the rear. More than 20 per cent of Chinese men of working age have degrees, as do nearly 20 per cent of Indian males, but this is true of fewer than ten per cent of black Caribbean and Pakistani males (whites fall midway between the two).[7] Not surprisingly given these figures, Indian and Chinese men are twice as likely as whites to be in professional jobs, and all three groups are twice as likely as Caribbean men to hold managerial positions.[8]

For the EHRC, ethnic differences in educational and occupational outcomes reflect the operation of a 'systemic bias' (institutional racism) in British society and institutions.[9] The Commission notes, for example, that ten per cent of black Caribbean people say they have been subject to discrimination by employers, but only one per cent of whites say this.[10] But it is difficult to see how racist practices, norms and structures could systematically disadvantage Pakistani and black Caribbean people, yet work to the positive advantage of Indians and Chinese, who commonly outperform whites in both the education system and in later careers.

Clearly these outcomes have little or nothing to do with racism in the education system. It is much more likely that they reflect cultural differences such as the high value Indian and Chinese parents typically place on education, and their commitment to strong, traditional family values which provide their children with a stable and supportive upbringing.[11] These are not explanations commonly favoured by those working in the equalities industry, however.

One major factor is almost certainly stable parenting.[12] More than half (54 per cent) of black Caribbean families in Britain are headed by single parents. This compares with 23 per cent of white families and just nine per cent of Indian families. Only a quarter of Caribbean children live with two parents. One result of this very high level of family breakdown in the black Caribbean population is a very high rate of welfare dependency (half of Caribbean one-parent families depend on welfare benefits), and a high rate of child poverty. Linked to this is the low level of school achievement, for we know that children's success at school correlates with the stability of their family circumstances at home.

Some black commentators have had the courage to recognise this and to acknowledge it publicly. Tony Sewell, who runs the charity Generating Genius, says: 'What we now see in schools is children undermined by poor parenting, peer-group pressure and an inability to be responsible for their own behaviour. They are not the subjects of institutional racism. They have failed their GCSEs because they did not do the homework, did not pay attention and were disrespectful to their teachers. Instead of challenging our children, we have given them the discourse of the victim—a sense that the world is against them and they cannot succeed.'[13] Unfortunately, voices like Sewell's are still too rarely heard.

Cognitive ability: social class, social mobility and university entrance

According to research by the Sutton Trust, half of Oxbridge admissions come from just 200 schools, many of which are in the private sector.[14] Forty per cent of the students at the country's top ten universities in 2006-7 were from private schools.[15]

The equalities industry is convinced these statistics indicate that unfair and class-biased selection procedures are being used by our top universities to favour the children of the rich and to keep lower-class kids out of higher education.[16] And it seems the government agrees with them. In 2010, David Willetts, the Universities Minister, urged universities to judge applicants, not on their A-level achievements, but on their 'potential'.[17] He wanted students from poor homes to be offered places on lower grades than those from more affluent backgrounds to make up for the disadvantages of their deprived upbringing, and he wanted universities to reduce the number of entrants they accept from private schools. He denied that this meant imposing quotas, but this is inevitably where such a policy would end up.

The following year, the government launched its new 'social mobility strategy'. This put the issue of university admissions at its core. Before they are allowed to raise their fees above £6,000, the government requires universities to submit to the Office of Fair Access clear plans for how they will attract more students from poorer backgrounds. Commitment to social engineering has thus become the price of higher education solvency, and Oxford announced it was willing to consider limiting the number of places it awards to candidates from private schools in order to comply with the government's demands. This policy is now being challenged by the Independent Schools Council which claims it breaches equalities law by discriminating unfairly against children on the basis of the schooling decisions made by their parents.[18]

It is unlikely that social class quotas on university admissions will achieve much even if they survive this legal test. In the past 50 years, many, much more dramatic reforms have been introduced to try to reduce the educational achievement gap between working-class and middle-class children, and none of them have worked. Two generations ago, middle-class children were three or four times more likely to get professional-managerial level jobs than children born to working-class parents, and this ratio is much the same today, despite the abolition of grammar schools, a quadrupling of higher education numbers, a dumbing down of examinations and repeated attempts at extending 'social inclusion' in education.[19]

The key reason for the persistence of this 'attainment gap' is that intelligence is unequally distributed across the social classes. Middle-class children are on average brighter than working class children, which is why they keep doing better at school and end up in larger numbers at university.

Equalities campaigners think this is an appalling thing to say, but it should not really shock or surprise us. Employers, after all, try to select the most talented people they can get. This means that the brightest people tend to end up in the top (middle-class) jobs where they often meet and marry other talented people. They then produce children who are more likely to be of above-average ability themselves. These children go through the education system, pass exams and wind up in top universities before going on to enter middle-class careers, thereby emulating the achievements of their parents.

The evidence for how ability drives social mobility can be found in the results from a study of over 17,000 people who were all born in one week in 1958. They have been followed through to adulthood, and the wealth of detail collected about them as they were growing up allow us to measure the contribution made by dozens of different factors to their eventual educational and occupational success. My analysis of this evidence shows that their social class origins did have some effect on where they ended up: whether you go to private or state school, what your parents do for a living, whether your parents take an active interest in your education, all of these things do have some influence on how well you do in life. But the significance of class background is eclipsed by the impact of just two personal characteristics: how hard you work, and how intelligent you are.[20]

If we divide the population into three broad, occupational classes, differentiated by income and levels of responsibility, half of us end up in a different class from the one we were born into. The main influence on whether we move up or down is our intelligence as measured by a simple IQ test taken at the age of 11. If you want to predict what class someone will end up in, knowing their IQ is three times more useful to you than knowing what class they were starting out from.

When ministers like Nick Clegg and David Willetts complain that middle-class children are 'over-represented' in our universities, they never ask whether differences of intellectual ability might have something to do with it. It is more comfortable for them to ignore intelligence differences and blame universities for class discrimination.[21]

Biological variation: Pakistani and black Caribbean infant mortality rates

One of the 'stark' variations the EHRC Fairness Report finds is the difference in infant mortality rates across different ethnic groups. The infant mortality rate for white British babies is 4.5 per thousand live births, while that for Pakistani babies is 9.8 per thousand—almost double. The black Caribbean rate is also troublingly high (9.6). Yet, counter-intuitively, the Bangladeshi rate is lower than that for white British babies at just 4.2.[22]

Following its own presumption that 'stark' differences 'must' be due to social conditions, the report gets understandably indignant about the Pakistani and black Caribbean figures (although it remains oddly incurious about the apparent Bangladeshi anomaly): 'The case for action is a moral one. We question whether a society committed to the principles of equality and human rights could be indifferent to such widely differing infant mortality rates among different groups.' The aim of 'closing the infant mortality gap' is duly instated as another of the Commission's priorities in its 'agenda for fairness'.

The data on infant mortality cited by the EHRC report come from the Office for National Statistics. But the ONS report which presents these findings also makes clear that: 'Half of all infant deaths in the Pakistani group were due to congenital abnormalities, compared with only a quarter of deaths in the white British group.'[23] Research published in the *British Medical Journal* suggests this high incidence of congenital abnormality is probably due to high rates of inter-marriage within extended Pakistani families.[24]

It always was unlikely that the high rate of infant mortality could have been due to the socio-economic conditions of Pakistani families, for these are quite similar to those of Bangladeshi families who enjoy an infant mortality rate less than half that of their Pakistani neighbours. What the *BMJ* article makes clear is that the defects causing these deaths are *genetic*. In most Asian populations throughout the world, the rate of congenital abnormalities in new-born babies is actually below the average for whites, but in the case of the UK Pakistani community, the prevalence of cousin marriages appears to have pushed this rate up.

This still leaves the question of the high black Caribbean infant mortality rate. But again, it seems genes are at the bottom of it. Research has found that black women in many countries are at greater risk of giving birth before reaching full term than white women (pre-term rates in the UK and USA are 16-18 per cent for blacks compared with 5-9 per cent for whites). This difference appears to be genetically determined and has nothing to do with socio-economic conditions.[25] Its relevance is that early births are associated with a higher risk of infant mortality.

To achieve the lower infant mortality rate it wants among Pakistanis, the EHRC would need to block cousin marriages, which would presumably bring it into conflict with its own principles of tolerating cultural differences. To achieve the lower rate it wants among black Caribbean women, it would have to start dabbling in some genetic engineering. Rather than allowing its 'moral outrage' to shape its aims and recommendations, the EHRC should try to understand that some 'stark' differences between ethnic groups can have biological foundations.

Distinctive behaviour patterns: ethnic minorities and the police

While black people make up just 2-3 per cent of the population, they constituted 15 per cent of those stopped and searched by the police in 2008-09.[26] Relative to their population size, the EHRC calculates that in 2007/08, black people were stopped and searched 6.5 times more than they 'should' have been, and Asians 1.9 times more. We saw in chapter 4 that it was these figures that led the Macpherson Report to its 'clear core conclusion of racist stereotyping' by police officers.[27]

But Macpherson was wrong. Consider Table 9.1. It shows that Thames Valley Police stop and search Asians in Reading twice as often as their numbers in the population would appear to warrant (five per cent of the population, ten per cent of stops), and blacks are stopped 2.5 times as often than they 'should' be (six per cent against 15 per cent). In nearby Slough, Asian stop and search figures look roughly 'right' (28 per cent against 31 per cent), but blacks are again stopped 2.5 times more frequently than they 'should' be (six per cent of the population, 15 per cent of stops). Alarmed by these figures, Thames Valley Policy commissioned independent criminologists to investigate the reasons behind this apparent persistent of 'institutional racism,' despite all their efforts to stamp it out.

Table 9.1: Ethnic patterns in police stop and search in Reading and Slough

	Reading			Slough		
	Pop %	Available pop %	Stop & search %	Pop %	Available pop %	Stop & search %
White	87	74	75	64	42	54
Black	6	13	15	6	17	15
Asian	5	9	10	28	40	31

Source: Extracted from Table 1 in P. Waddington, K., Stenson and D., Don, 'In proportion: race, and police stop and search', *British Journal of Criminology*, vol. 44, 2004.

What the researchers found was that in both towns, blacks and Asians were spending more time than whites in public places, on foot or in cars, where they were 'available' to be selected by the police for stop and search. Using their own observations and CCTV footage, the researchers compared police stop and search records with the number of people in different ethnic groups who were out and about in areas patrolled by the police. They discovered that in Reading, all ethnic groups were stopped and searched in proportion to their numbers on the streets, and that in Slough, whites were actually over-represented in the police stop and search statistics while Asians were under-represented. In other words, if you spend time driving around the streets or hanging out in the pedestrian precinct, you are more likely to attract the attention of passing police patrols, irrespective of your ethnicity.

As a result of doing this research, the team also came to realise how difficult it would be in many situations for racist police officers to determine the ethnicity of somebody before stopping them. In a car in good day-light, the researchers were able to determine the ethnicity of the occupants of other cars around them in only five per cent of cases. Pedestrian ethnicity too is often hard to pick. If the police were targeting suspects according to their ethnicity, we should expect ethnic minorities to be stopped more in circumstances where it is easier for the police to determine their racial characteristics (e.g. at times of day when the light is better, or in summer, when people wear fewer clothes that obscure their skin colour and features). But when the researchers checked this, they found no difference.

They concluded that in the Thames Valley force at least, there is simply no evidence that the police are using their stop and search powers to target ethnic minorities unfairly. Each group is being stopped in proportion to its availability. As for Macpherson, their findings could not be clearer: 'Macpherson was in error in concluding that the disproportionality in stop and search figures was evidence of racial stereotyping.'[28]

It is also important to look at what happens after somebody is stopped and searched. The EHRC reports that the police arrest about one in ten of all those they stop and search, but this is true across all the ethnic groups.[29] Thus, although blacks are being stopped more often by the police, they are also more often found to be engaged in activities that turn out to warrant an arrest. Once again, there is no evidence from these figures that they are being unfairly targeted.

Blacks are five times more likely than whites to find themselves in prison, and equalities campaigners often cite this as evidence that our law and order system is biased. The EHRC, for example, is indignant that ethnic minorities make up 25 per cent of the prison population when they only account for 11 per cent of the population as a whole (a 'greater disproportionality in the number of black people in prisons in the UK than in the United States).[30] But it offers no data on the ethnic composition of *offenders*. The possibility that there are more black people in prison because more black people commit crimes is rarely considered in this literature. To the EHRC, it seems to be unthinkable, racist even.

In 2007, a Home Affairs Committee Report looked into the reasons why young black people are over-represented at all stages of the criminal justice system.[31] It said it is 'unclear whether young black people commit more crime of all types than young people as a whole,' although it accepted compelling evidence that 'they are more likely overall to be involved in certain types of serious and violent crime, including gun crime'. It also found evidence of higher levels of black involvement in criminal gangs and drug crime. Yet despite this, it could not bring itself to accept the possibility that higher imprisonment figures reflect higher offending rates. The report concluded that: 'Social exclusion—both historic and current—is the key, primary cause of young black people's overrepresentation' in arrest and imprisonment statistics, and it repeated familiar accusations about police bias in stop and search procedures.[32]

The Coalition Government is also very sensitive about this issue. Its Equality Strategy notes that the National DNA Database contains a disproportionate number of young black men. It accepts that more blacks than whites are convicted of offences, but it worries that black arrest rates are higher than black conviction rates. It therefore promises to eradicate this 'unfairness' by removing from the database the DNA of all people who have been arrested but not convicted.[33] What effect this will have on future detection rates is anybody's guess.

When victims outperform oppressors

The Coalition Government is in no doubt that the various 'protected groups' in Britain are getting a raw deal. In its Equality Strategy, it cites differences in men's and women's average pay, different unemployment rates in different ethnic groups, and relatively low rates of employment of disabled people.[34] It also identifies as examples of 'unequal opportunities' the fact that children born to lower-class parents tend to end up in worse jobs than those born to higher-class parents; the fact that black Caribbean and Pakistani babies have higher infant mortality rates than Bangladeshi or white babies; the fact that gypsy children get fewer GCSEs than other children; and the fact that black Caribbean students are three times more likely to be excluded from school than white students. All such evidence is taken to indicate that 'many opportunities remain closed to the disadvantaged'.[35]

As we have seen, in many of these cases there are factors other than discrimination and disadvantage which the Equality Strategy overlooks but which better explain the outcomes it is worried about. But like the rest of the equalities industry, the authors of the Equality Strategy are only interested in contextual explanations, not compositional ones, and for them, evidence of unequal outcomes is all that is necessary to 'prove' the existence of discrimination or systemic bias.

This might not be quite so bad if they were at least consistent in the application of this logic. But they are not. Whenever unequal outcomes seem to favour mainstream groups over protected ones (men over women, blacks over whites, heterosexuals over gays), they are seized upon as conclusive evidence of bias. But sometimes these inequalities run in the opposite direction, favouring protected groups over mainstream ones. And when this happens, a veil is drawn over the whole discussion.

From the EHRC report's, *How Fair Is Britain?*, we find that Chinese men and women report the best health, not whites. Indeed, black African men living in Britain report better health on average than white British men do.[36] What are we to conclude from this? The EHRC declines to comment.

Indian and Chinese men are also twice as likely as white British men to be in professional jobs,[37] and Indian people are more likely than whites to be in the professional/managerial class.[38] Children from Asian families are less likely to be excluded from school than children from white families.[39] When they come to take their GCSEs, Indian and Chinese pupils comfortably out-perform everybody else, while white children do no better than Bangladeshi or black children.[40] White pupils report higher levels of bullying than pupils from ethnic minorities, and as adults, whites are more likely to be victims of violence.[41] Blacks and Asians also seem to feel more empowered than whites.[42]

Evidence like this obviously casts doubt on the equality industry's favoured explanation for ethnic differences, which has to do with so-called 'systemic bias' in British society and institutions.[43] It is difficult to see how racist practices, or systematically exclusionary norms and structures, could keep disadvantaging Pakistanis while at the same time working to the positive advantage of Indians. Nor is it obvious how a systemically racist society could produce so many examples of white British people performing worse than Indian or Chinese people (although some Marxist academics have made heroic attempts to present Asian children's 'over-performance' in school as a distorted product of 'institutional racism'!).[44] When outcomes for whites are better than those for, say, Pakistani or Afro-Caribbean people, it is assumed that we have encountered some 'unfairness' that needs remedying. When the statistics are the other way around, however, everyone just stays silent.

A good example of this double standard can be found in a 2009 report on ethnic minorities in the NHS. The report found that, while 15 per cent of people employed by the National Health Service are black or from other ethnic minorities, this was true of only ten per cent of senior managers, and only one per cent of trust chief executives. This was immediately recognised as a cause for concern and grounds for remedial action. The Department of Health's equality and human rights 'tsar' told the *Guardian* that he was working with the Cabinet Office to introduce 'targets' to reduce this 'white domination of top jobs,' and the EHRC welcomed any 'positive action' that would 'enable black and ethnic minority staff to compete for jobs on a level playing field'.[45]

Yet the same report also found that 25 per cent of consultants, and 47 per cent of registrars, were black or minority ethnic. This would appear to be a clear 'over-representation' of minority groups in the ranks of senior medics, but neither the NHS diversity Tsar nor the EHRC thought this merited any comment at all.

We saw in chapter 8 that when men are found to outnumber women among hospital consultants, it's seen by the equalities industry as a clear case of discrimination. So why does blacks outnumbering whites in the same profession produce no such reaction? Similarly, when this report finds whites are statistically over-represented among NHS managers, it sees it as evidence that targets and quotas are needed to provide a 'level playing field'; but when blacks are found to be statistically over-represented among consultants, no equivalent con-clusions are drawn.

Clearly, statistical evidence on outcomes gets selectively cherry-picked to suit whichever argument equalities campaigners want to make.

It is the same with statistics on gender differences where again the supposedly 'dominant' group is often found to be worse off than its 'victims'. In the EHRC fairness report, we can find statistics showing that women typically live four years longer than men.[46] Men are also typically more overweight,[47] are more likely to commit suicide,[48] get assaulted more,[49] and are killed at work in much greater numbers.[50] Men, furthermore, are much more likely than women to be stopped and searched by the police,[51] and 95 per cent of prisoners are male.[52] But none of this is thought to represent evidence of 'unfairness' or 'discrimination', and none of it leads equalities campaigners to the conclusion that something drastic needs to be done to rectify the gender imbalance. Outcomes are only unfair when the equalities industry decides they are unfair.

10

What Is To Be Done?

In the 1960s, when the UK government took its first faltering steps towards outlawing racial discrimination, it was clear that the country faced a real problem regarding equal treatment of all citizens under the law, and it was important to have new legislation to help deal with this.

Almost half a century later, when Harriet Harman bulldozed her 2010 Equality Bill through the House of Commons, this original problem had abated. The days when restaurants might refuse to serve black customers, or when employers could get away with paying female workers a lower rate for doing exactly the same job, had long since passed into memory. But this did not deter Harriet Harman. Faced with a much smaller problem today, she wanted a much bigger stick to deal with it. Boosted by a few misleading statistics and a messianic belief in the justice of her cause, she saddled Britain with a huge and ugly slab of legislation which, we have seen, is unnecessary, costly and destructive.

At the time this Bill was going through Parliament, the Conservative opposition made no attempt to stop it. But now the Conservative Party is back in power, albeit in coalition with the Liberal Democrats, it has taken one or two worthwhile if small steps back from its worst excesses.

The section of the 2010 Equality Act which extended the public sector equality duty to cover socio-economic background has, for example, been scrapped, although this still leaves us with the nine protected identities in tact. There has also been a modest attempt to modify the nature of the public sector equality duty in the hope of reducing the monitoring workload; the bloated EHRC is being halved in size and stripped of its responsibility for 'promoting good relations'; and we are promised some reform of employment tribunals to deter people from bringing non-serious cases. All of this should be welcomed.

But for every positive move, the government is also making a negative one. It has published its own, vacuous 'Equalities Strategy' which reinforces rather than challenges the equalities orthodoxy by accepting evidence of differential group outcomes as proof of unfairness and discrimination, when it is not. It is also pushing companies to introduce gender pay audits, threatening to force them with new laws if they do not comply voluntarily, and it is dabbling dangerously with quotas (although like the last government, it tries to maintain the pretence that targets are different from quotas). Companies are being told to increase the number of women directors appointed to their boards, and universities are being told to squeeze the number of applicants they accept from private schools. For a government which claims to be committed to the ideal of devolved power, this one is doing a lot of centralising in the name of equality.

Ideally, what this government should be doing is fundamentally revising the 2010 Equality Act with the idea of reinforcing and safeguarding the principle of formal equality. It is tempting to suggest that the whole Act should simply be repealed, but it would be a mistake to lose the safeguards against direct race and sex discrimination which were laid down in the 1960s and 1970s. As we saw in chapter 3, there is a strong case for a law to protect people against discrimination based on their sex or race, for these are basic roles which they can do little to disguise or change. Those aspects of the disability legislation requiring public premises and public transport to improve accessibility where this is reasonable should also be retained.

But the mistake we made from the mid-seventies onwards was to extend statutory protections to other groups who should not need them, while also muddying the definition of what discrimination entails by introducing concepts like 'indirect discrimination' and 'institutionalised racism' without regard for people's intentions or motives. It is these errors that desperately need rectifying.

A sensible equalities law would therefore retain a simple ban on direct race and sex discrimination, and would keep disability access rules for transport and public places, but beyond that it would:

- limit 'protected groups' to those defined by gender or ethnic identities only, and scrap statutory protections for groups based on age, sexuality, disability and religion/belief (this would effectively take us back to the situation prior to 1995);

- insist that any claim of discrimination or unfairness on grounds of sex or race should require evidence of unfair processes, and should not rest solely on a statistical analysis of differential group outcomes;

- limit the definition of 'indirect discrimination' to situations where there is evidence of an intent to use a common set of rules to exclude people on the basis of their race or sex;

- restrict the use of terms like 'institutional racism' or 'systemic bias' to refer to the documented existence of rules or formal procedures in organisations which can be shown to operate to the advantage of one gender or ethnic group and to the disadvantage of another;

- limit equal pay legislation to people doing the same jobs, and end the time-consuming, fatuous and acrimonious pretence of pay audits claiming to establish whether different jobs are of 'comparable value';

- explicitly ban the use of any quotas or targets in the public sector which improve or diminish the selection chances of individuals from any social group, and reassert an unequivocal commitment to meritocratic recruitment criteria across the state sector;

- scrap the 'equality duty' on organisations to monitor and publish their staffing or customer profiles (for not only does this represent a massive waste of money and time, but the information will no longer be needed if indirect discrimination is redefined as suggested above);

- scrap the requirement that new policies be the subject of an equality impact assessment;

- if not abolishing the Equalities and Human Rights Commission, then limit its duties to supporting formal equality on grounds of race and sex, scrap its responsibility for 'promoting' equality, and curtail its power to hand out grants to special interest advocacy groups;

- wind up other equalities and diversity quangos, including the Government Equalities Office and the

Office for Fair Access, and close equality and diversity units in government departments, the NHS and other public sector agencies;

- scrap special penalties for 'hate crimes,' and make explicit a universal right of free speech (including the right to cause offence provided this does not involve intent to cause a breach of the peace); and

- require unsuccessful employment tribunal plaintiffs to meet their own and their employer's full costs.

Unfortunately, little of this can or will be done, for two reasons.

One has to do with European law. We have seen that many of the recent extensions to our equalities laws did not originate on the floor of the House of Commons, but were imposed as a result of European directives from Brussels. This was true of the extension of protection on the basis of sexual orientation and religion and belief, both in 2003, and the introduction of age discrimination legislation (including the ban on forcible retirement at 65) in 2006. Moreover, even the laws which we did come up with ourselves are now underpinned by the European Court and the Human Rights Act, so while we may have introduced them, we no longer have the power to rescind them. And to make matters worse, there is plenty more European equalities legislation that is going to hit us in the future (it seems likely, for example, that Europe will impose statutory gender quotas for company boards at some point in the next few years, which Westminster will then feel bound to implement).

However, while European sovereignty over the UK limits our reform options, it does not curtail them altogether. It may not be possible under European law to reduce the number of protected groups, for example, but it should still be possible to change some of the definitions and procedures. Rescinding the duty on public bodies to promote equality, scrapping the equality impact assessments on new policies, scaling down or winding up the EHRC, repealing the hate crimes legislation and changing the definition and measurement of 'discrimination' to end the reliance on statistical outcomes and to tighten the identification of cases of indirect and systemic discrimination, all this should still be possible. The government should investigate the options which are available to it and bring forward reform proposals as a matter of priority.

But this brings us to the second reason why these proposals are unlikely to be acted upon, which is that many of our politicians appear in thrall to the equalities industry and are scared to move against it. It is not just that equalities advocates now represent a strong and well-established interest group which can make life extremely uncomfortable for anyone who challenges them — although this certainly weighs heavily with politicians who generally prefer a quiet life over public confrontation and recrimination. It is also that the language of 'equality' has been captured by these people, and this makes it extremely difficult for anybody now to move against them.

For 50 years, the equalities industry in Britain has been on the front foot, driving forward its definitions of 'fairness' in terms of equal outcomes, and chipping away at the liberal ideal of formal equality. Almost nobody has stood up to it during this period, so resistance to its ideas and objectives now that the industry has established itself in thousands of different organisations across the country will be that much more difficult. Any political challenge will almost certainly be met by loud and vociferous claims that opponents of the equalities industry are seeking to defend 'unfairness' and reinforce 'privilege'. Such claims can only be countered by a vigorous defence of the alternative, liberal conception of fairness which emphasises the principle of equal treatment under a common set of rules, and which is therefore concerned with processes rather than outcomes.

Politicians whose instinct is to ally with the equalities industry, rather than mounting a robust challenge to its growing influence and hegemony, should understand that it is not some neutral force for good in British politics. We have seen that it has its own, anti-liberal agenda, championing group identity over individual responsibility and equality of outcomes over equality before the law. As David Green suggests: 'No doubt there are many naive champions of victim groups who think they are simply being "nice", but it is no coincidence that many activists of the hard left who previously tried to inflame class divisions have switched their attention to victim groups as potentially more promising sources of hostility to liberalism.'[1] The rhetoric on their banners may still refer to equality, but unlike the French and American revolutionaries of the eighteenth century, their agenda today is not the defence of liberal capitalism, but its dismantling.

Back in the 1920s, the Italian Marxist Antonio Gramsci realised that the industrial proletariat was never going to overthrow capitalism, as Marx had promised, and that the capitalist economic system was certainly not going to collapse under the weight of its own historical contradictions, as Marx had prophesised. Gramsci therefore proposed that a long class war against capitalism should be fought, not in the factories, but in and across the cultural institutions of modern societies—the schools, the media, the family, the churches and any other institutions which play a part in maintaining and reproducing a society's sense of itself and its core values. The aim was to 'transform popular consciousness' by fostering a 'revolutionary counter-hegemony'. In plain language, capitalism could be subverted from the inside, and intellectuals would play the leading role in undermining the foundations.[2]

Gramsci's ideas became popular among young radicals in the 1960s, and ever since then, the west has been embroiled in what have aptly been called a series of 'culture wars' around myriad issues of personal morality and civic life.[3] In Britain, the principal battles have been fought around the institution of marriage, support for single parenthood, the moral authority of traditional religion, traditional versus progressive education, the spread of recreational drug use and other hedonistic lifestyles once limited to a Bohemian minority, 'progressive' arts funding and the control of the BBC, the morality of unconditional welfare rights, acceptance for alternative sexualities, green politics and environmentalism—and the pursuit of end-state 'equality'. The social affairs intellectuals of the UK equalities industry have been in the vanguard of this cultural battle, eroding the ideals of independent thought, self-reliance and personal responsibility and replacing them with the language of thought-crime, group rights and equal outcomes.[4]

Since the 1960s, as these culture wars have been progressing, so the equalities industry has moved from 'outsider' to 'insider' status, and from the defensive to the offensive. Fifty years ago, the aim was simply to achieve tolerance for diversity—e.g. by decriminalising consensual acts of homosexuality in private, or by stopping pubs and restaurants from imposing colour bars. This was an agenda consistent with classical liberalism. But today, emboldened by their acceptance into the heart of the British establishment,[5] radical egalitarians seek nothing less than hegemony for their moral values and beliefs, and this requires the unconditional surrender of their adversaries. It is no longer sufficient that homosexuality should be tolerated for example; now the aim is to criminalise those who oppose it.

Egalitarians seek to establish their hegemony by writing their morality into the law of the land and into the rulebooks of every organisation of civil society. They can then use this institutional power to purge their opponents. If you have been wondering, ever since chapter 1, why the equalities industry always seems to side with the atheists against the Presbyterians, or with the gays against the Pentacostalists, then here is your answer. Despite the rhetoric, modern equalities discourse is not neutral. It is tied to a wider and deeper political agenda, and it is bent to its purpose. If this agenda is not opposed with a clearly-articulated, alternative conception of fairness rooted in the liberal tradition of equal treatment under a single set of rules, then liberalism itself will eventually crumble and fade away.

Harman's Equality Act was a key moment in the UK culture wars. It institutionalised and consolidated all the equality industry's victories of the last 40 years, brought all the 'protected identities' together under a common, unifying umbrella of victim rights, and reinforced the ideal of equality of outcomes as the only legitimate test of 'fairness'. But it is still not too late to challenge this creeping hegemony. New public attitudes research published in April 2011 reveals that, despite 50 years of this equalities onslaught, most people in Britain still reject core elements in the equality industry's way of thinking.

The repeated claim that Britain is an 'unfair' society has, unsurprisingly, had some impact on popular belief and sentiment. Asked 'How fair do you think Britain is today?', only 42 per cent of the population says it is very or mostly fair, while 51 per cent say it is very or mostly unfair. But the crucial attempt by the equalities industry to link conceptions of fairness to equality of outcomes does not attract strong support. Asked, for example, if 'you can have a fair society even though people's incomes are quite unequal', 73 per cent of people thought that you could, and only 18 per cent denied it. And responding to the classic statement of the egalitarian position, 'In a fair society, nobody should get an income a lot bigger or a lot smaller than anybody else gets', 41 per cent agreed, but 50 per cent did not.[6]

There are also hopeful signs that some equalities intellectuals are themselves wearying of the dominant mode of discourse and are reasserting the liberal conception of fairness as equal treatment under the law. In October 2010, the left-of-centre *Prospect* magazine ran a special issue on 'Rethinking Race' in which four British intellectuals, all from ethnic minority backgrounds, questioned current equality and diversity orthodoxy.

Introducing this issue, Munira Mirza cited evidence on the educational attainment, criminality and social mobility rates of groups like the Indians and Chinese to support her claim that: 'race is no longer the significant disadvantage it is often portrayed to be'. She identified a climate of fear and paternalism surrounding any discussion of race in this country, and she attacked the way the 'equality duty' on public sector organisations has spawned an army of 'ethnic monitors, diversity trainers and equality impact assessors' who achieve little other than creating a 'climate of suspicion and anxiety'.[7]

Mirza is right, and what she says of race applies to all the other protected groups as well. Now all we need to do is convince Mr Cameron.

Notes

1: What Kind of Equality?

1   Rod Liddle, 'If Western Islanders want miserable Sundays, what right have the rest of us to interfere?', *Spectator*, 5 February 2011, p. 21.

2   Neil Midgley, 'Middle class, white Radio 4 told to appeal to minorities', *Daily Telegraph*, 9 February 2011.

3   The assumption, presumably, was that the high-brow, London-based, culture and current affairs stuff would never appeal to simple working-class folk from the north, but they might be enticed to come to a recording of a programme about gardening or eating. Much equalities policy and practice is highly patronising. Black children are assumed to need a different curriculum to interest them in school work; female artists need special exhibitions and prizes; working-class listeners need special programmes and events; and so on. See Sanya Dyer, 'Wanted: A new image', *Prospect*, October 2010, pp. 36-37.

4   Some critics suggested ethnic quotas on 'talent' would water down standards. Others said that widening the appeal of Radio 4 would destroy what is distinctive about the station. The truth is, Radio 4 is aimed at the educated middle class, and today, such an admission is seen as a problem that requires rectifying. See Rod Liddle, 'Radio 4 "lowers standards for racial reasons"', *Sunday Times*, 13 February 2011.

5   A good example of this occurred at Harvard in 2005 when the President, Larry Summers, suggested that the continuing male domination of science (despite years of gender equity initiatives in schools and universities) may reflect a difference in average cognitive skills between men and women. His comments triggered an extraordinary backlash by academics, Summers was forced into a humiliating

retraction, and Harvard introduced gender quotas in science faculties to placate the critics. A year later, Summers resigned. See Charles Murray, 'Sex, science and economics', *The American Enterprise,* June 2005, pp. 26-28.

6 T. H. Marshall, *Citizenship and Social Class, and Other Essays,* Cambridge University Press, 1950.

7 In a 2011 public opinion survey commissioned by Policy Exchange, 85% of Britons agreed with the proposition that: 'In a fair society, people's incomes should depend on how hard they work and how talented they are', and only 8% disagreed. Neil O'Brien, 'Just deserts? Attitudes to fairness, poverty and welfare reform', Policy Exchange *Research Note,* April 2011.

8 Even with the introduction of higher university fees, there are exemptions for students from poor backgrounds, and nobody has to start paying until they start earning a reasonable salary after graduation.

9 Peter Saunders, *Social Mobility Myths,* Civitas, 2010.

10 That the key advantages are cultural, not financial, can be seen in the extraordinary levels of success achieved by Chinese and Indian children in British schools (see chapter 9). Many lack the material advantages of their white contemporaries, but what they have is strong families and committed parents who value education and want their children to succeed. This sort of 'cultural capital' cannot be redistributed by governments.

11 For egalitarians, talent is a quirk of birth, so people with particular abilities do not deserve the rewards which these abilities can generate. The willingness to work hard can also be dismissed as a product of genetic endowment or early socialisation, and either way, it cannot therefore be claimed as moral grounds for additional reimbursement. The philosophical basis of these arguments was provided by

John Rawls, *A Theory of Justice*, New York: Basic Books, 1974. See also Gordon Marshall, Adam Swift and Stephen Roberts, *Against the Odds? Social Class and Social Justice in Industrial Societies*, Clarendon Press, 1997.

12 Karl Marx, 'Critique of the Gotha Programme', in Marx and Engels *Selected Works in One Volume*, Lawrence & Wishart 1968.

13 Richard Wilkinson and Kate Pickett, *The Spirit Level: Why Equality is Better for Everyone*, Penguin, 2010.

14 The argument and evidence are critically examined in Peter Saunders, *Beware False Prophets*, Policy Exchange, 2010; (second edition, *When Prophecy Fails*, published by Centre for Independent Studies, Sydney, 2011); and Christopher Snowdon, *The Spirit Level Delusion*, Little Dice, 2010.

15 F.A. Hayek, *The Constitution of Liberty*, Routledge and Kegan Paul, 1960, p. 87.

16 HM Government, *The Equality Strategy: building a fairer Britain*, December 2010, p. 6.

17 *The Equality Strategy: building a fairer Britain*, p. 8.

18 *The Equality Strategy: building a fairer Britain*, p. 5.

19 *The Equality Strategy: building a fairer Britain*, p. 6.

20 I discuss this in Peter Saunders, 'Must all students now pass the Nick Clegg test?', *Daily Telegraph*, 9 February 2011.

21 Andrew Porter and others, 'Cameron brands 'all-white' Oxford a disgrace', *Daily Telegraph*, 12 April 2011.

22 Peter Lampl, whose Sutton Trust has been driving most of these demands for preferential entry criteria for poor applicants, says: 'It beggars belief that we demand the same A-level grades from a pupil at an inner city comprehensive as from a pupil at a top state or private school', in 'Forget

costly UK universities. Go to America', *The Times*, 12 July 2011. Formal equality beggars belief?

23 *The Equality Strategy: building a fairer Britain*, p. 7.

2: Too Much of a Good Thing?

1   Under common law, it was unlawful for an hotel to turn away an overnight guest on grounds of race, or for a common carrier to refuse him/her transport, but all other forms of discrimination were legal: see B. Hepple, 'Race Relations Act 1965', *The Modern Law Review*, vol. 29, 1966, pp. 306-14.

2   Migration Watch UK, *The History of Migration to the UK*, 2001;
    http://www.migrationwatchuk.com/pdfs/6_1_History_of_im
    migration.pdf

3   Sheila Patterson, *Dark Strangers*, London: Tavistock, 1963.

4   Sarah Dar, 'Facing the colour bar';
    http://www.connectinghistories.org.uk/Learning%20Packag
    es/Migration/migration_settlement_20c_lp_02b.asp

5   John Rex and Robert Moore, *Race Community and Conflict*, Oxford University Press, 1967.

6   In the event, only five cases were referred to the Attorney General in the two-and-a-half-years that the Act was in force. One hundred and nine cases referred to the Board were not sustained, and 65 were settled by conciliation. B. Hepple, 'Race Relations Act 1968', *The Modern Law Review*, vol. 32, 1969, pp. 181-86.

7   B. Hepple, 'Race Relations Act 1965', p. 314.

8   Race Relations Act 1968, London: HMSO, chapter 71.

9 'Bristol gay couple win B&B Cornwall bed ban case', BBC News, http://www.bbc.co.uk/news/uk-england-bristol-12214368. The insistence that couples who share a room should be married was held to be unlawfully discriminatory against gay couples. In chapter 3, I consider this issue in more detail.

10 The Scottish Social Attitudes Survey in 2006 found that 51% of people think someone suffering depression would be unsuitable as a primary school teacher, and 49% thought somebody over the age of 70 would be unsuitable (C. Bromley, J. Curtice and L. Given, 'Attitudes to discrimination in Scotland', *Research Findings* No.1, 2007, Scottish Centre for Social Research). It is, however, illegal for either of these factors to be taken into account in an employment decision.

11 The Scottish social attitudes survey, for example, finds that 51% of people think a B&B owner should be allowed to refuse a booking to a same-sex couple, even though this became unlawful in 2007 (C. Bromley, J. Curtice and L. Given, 'Attitudes to discrimination in Scotland'). Almost one-third also think B&B owners should be allowed to turn away youths, 21% think equality laws for gays and lesbians have 'gone too far', and 23% think the same for blacks and Asians. More than a third think it is wrong for companies to provide female employees with additional training to help them gain promotion, 41% think this is wrong in the case of ethnic minorities, and 57% oppose inclusion of a disabled candidate on a shortlist simply because of their disability. Meanwhile, in England and Wales, 26% of people think the government is doing too much to protect religious people's rights, while 27% think it is doing too little (Chris Ferguson and David Hussey, *2008-09 Citizenship Survey: Race, Religion and Equalities Topic Report*, London: Communities and Local Government, September 2010, Figure 3.7).

3: Too Many Victims

1   Equal Pay Act 1970, London: HMSO, chapter 41. In 1983, the legislation was broadened to include jobs of 'equal value' or 'comparable worth', and this has resulted in the growth of 'pay audits' in the public sector. Job evaluation schemes award different tasks points (e.g. for exercise of autonomy, skill, experience required, etc.), and jobs with the same score must be paid at the same rates, irrespective of supply and demand. See J. Shackleton, *Should We Mind the Gap?*, Institute of Economic Affairs, 2008, chapter 7.

2   Industrial tribunals, renamed employment tribunals in 1998, were established in 1964 to investigate complaints arising from employment law; they consist of an independent chairman sitting on a panel with one employer and one trades union representative.

3   M. Rendel, 'Legislating for equal pay and opportunity for women in Britain', *Signs*, vol.3, pp. 897-908.

4   Sex Discrimination Act 1975, London: HMSO, chapter 65.

5   A man was taken on in 1991 as manager at an education establishment in Cornwall. The following year he announced he was having gender reassignment and took sick leave. When she wished to resume her duties, the employer made her redundant. She went to a tribunal, claiming sex discrimination, and lost, but the matter was referred to the European Court of Justice which ruled that Directive 76/207/EEC, prohibiting sex discrimination, also precludes dismissal of transsexuals undergoing gender reassignment. 'P *vs* S: full record of the ECJ proceedings' http://www.pfc.org.uk/node/362

6   Disability Discrimination Act 1995.

7 N. Meager and D. Hill, 'The labour market participation and employment of disabled people in the UK', Institute of Employment Studies, *Working Paper* 1, 2005, p. 4.

8 Brian Doyle, 'Enabling legislation or Dissembling law?' *The Modern Law Review*, vol. 60, 1997, pp. 64-78.

9 *The Employment Equality (Religion or Belief) Regulations 2003,* Statutory Instrument No. 1660. *The Employment Equality (Sexual Orientation) Regulations 2003,* Statutory Instrument No. 1661.

10 *The Employment Equality (Age) Regulations 2006,* Statutory Instrument No. 1031.

11 Age UK, 'Forced retirement to be scrapped'; http://www.ageuk.org.uk/latest-news/archive/forced-retirement-to-be-scrapped/

12 The government anticipated 8,000 additional employment tribunal cases per year as a result of scrapping the compulsory retirement rule: Department of Trade and Industry, *Employment Equality (Age) Regulations 2006, Regulatory Impact Assessments* March 2006, p. 18.

13 It was reported in March 2011 that the Coalition government intends to remove the EHRC's responsibility for promoting 'good relations' between the various groups for which it is responsible. The government believes that much of the money the Commission has spent in discharging this duty has been wasted. 'Role of equalities watchdog curbed', *Daily Telegraph*, 23 March 2011.

14 Equality Act 2006, chapter 3, Explanatory notes.

15 Equality Act 2010, chapter 2.

16 Discriminating against someone with a poorly-spelled letter of application could be unlawful if there are grounds for believing they are dyslexic;

http://www.smarta.com/advice/legal/employment-law/the-equality-act-(october-1-2010)-need-to-know-for-small-businesses?gclid=CNa0ifLz0qcCFUtC4QodLxvd8g

17 Draft Statutory Instruments, 2011, no. xxx, *Equality: The Equality Act 2010 (Statutory Duties) Regulations 2011*, Schedule 1. The Race Relations (Amendment) Act of 2000 placed public bodies under a legal obligation to promote racial equality, which effectively meant they had to monitor their employment practices and their relations with the public so they could demonstrate progress. This was then reinforced by the 2006 Act.

18 Government Equalities Office, *Public Sector Equality Duty*; http://www.equalities.gov.uk/equality_act_2010/faqs_on_the _equality_act_2010/public_sector_equality_duty.aspx

19 HM Government, *The Equality Strategy: building a fairer Britain*, December 2010, p. 6.

20 David G. Green, *We're (Nearly) All Victims Now!*, Civitas, 2006, Table 1. This calculation was based on the 2006 Act. Other protected statuses have been added since.

21 For example: Michael Banton, *Roles*, Tavistock, 1965.

22 The race discrimination laws introduced in the 1960s also outlawed discrimination on the basis of nationality, and this has been carried over into the 2010 Equality Act. But the arguments justifying protection on grounds of race and sex seem less compelling when applied to national identities, and this part of the race discrimination laws may need rethinking. When he was Prime Minister, Gordon Brown called for 'British jobs' to be given to 'British workers', and more recently, Work and Pensions Secretary Iain Duncan Smith told employers they should give preference to British applicants when filling job vacancies, but in both cases, if employers were to follow the politicians' advice, they would be liable to claims for direct race discrimination. See Jason

Beattie, 'Tories' British jobs for British workers plan is racist, employers warn', *Daily Record*, 2 July 2011.

23 The baby boomers have also benefited from final salary pension schemes which the cohort behind them is going to have to finance, even though such schemes are increasingly closed to them. For discussion of this and other examples of cohort inequity, see David Willetts, *The Pinch: how the baby boomers took their children's future — and why they should give it back*, Atlantic Books, 2010, esp. chapter 4.

24 Figures from the 2008 *Family Resources Survey* and 2009 *Labour Force Survey*, reported by the Employers' Forum on Disability; http://www.efd.org.uk/media-centre/facts-and-figures/disability-in-uk

25 The government is reassessing the work capability of all claimants of disability payments. Under the new capability criteria, three-quarters of new claimants have been found to be capable of working. Andrew Porter, 'Three-quarters of benefits applicants capable of working', *Daily Telegraph*, 27 October 2010.

26 Robert Wintemute ('Recognising new kinds of direct sex discrimination', *The Modern Law Review*, vol. 60, 1997, pp. 334-59) suggests there is no 'conceptual' difference between sex discrimination involving men and women, and discrimination against transsexuals and cross-dressers. The only difference, he says, is that the latter represent a small minority of the population. But this ignores the fundamental difference between an ascribed attribute and a freely-selected behaviour.

27 Interestingly, as this book was going to press, I was asked to participate in a BBC radio discussion of the issues raised by the murder of 20-year-old Goth, Sophie Lancaster (*The Black Roses Debate*, Radio 4, 24 August 2011). Sophie's mother is campaigning to have crimes motivated by hatred of

someone's lifestyle added to the list of 'hate crimes', and many of the activists gathered in the studio to listen to the debate agreed with this. To hear the debate, go to: http://www.petersaunders.org.uk/radio_4_240811.html

28 M. Bell, 'A patchwork of protection: The new anti-discrimination law framework', *The Modern Law Review*, vol. 67, May 2004, p. 468.

29 Bell, 'A patchwork of protection', p. 468.

30 Tim Ross, 'Judges back fostering ban on "anti-gay" Christians', *Daily Telegraph*, 1 March 2011; Joshua Rozenberg, 'Jurisprudence', *Standpoint*, no. 31, April 2011, p. 23. As this book was going to press, however, two Roman Catholic nurses used the 2010 Equality Act to claim successfully that they were being victimised by the NHS for their 'philosophical beliefs' by being deployed to work in an abortion clinic. Their lawyer described their victory as 'a rare example of equality laws being used to protect the rights of Christians' (quoted in Tom Ross, 'Victory for the Catholic nurses who refused to work in abortion clinic', *Daily Telegraph*, 13 August 2011).

31 Tim Ross, 'Chief Rabbi: Equality laws leading to new Mayflower exodus', *Daily Telegraph*, 30 June 2011.

4: We Are All Guilty

1 Sex Discrimination Act 1975, chapter 65, Part I.

2 All these examples are taken from Thompsons Solicitors, *Summary of the law on sex discrimination*; www.thompsons.law.co.uk

3 In a recent case, the High Court ruled that an Afro-Caribbean pupil who had been sent home from school because his cornrow hairstyle broke school rules was the victim of 'unlawful, indirect discrimination.' Matthew

Taylor, 'School's ban on boy's cornrows is indirect racial discrimination', *Guardian*, 17 June 2011.

4   Aina v Employment Service 2002, details on EHRC website.

5   Norman Dennis, *Racist Murder and Pressure Group Politics*, Civitas, 2000, pp. 95-96.

6   The history of the case is recounted in detail by Norman Dennis, *Racist Murder and Pressure Group Politics*. In 2011, two of the men originally accused of the murder were re-arrested and at the time of writing are awaiting another trial (this follows the scrapping of the double jeopardy law).

7   Dennis, *Racist Murder and Pressure Group Politics*, p. 114.

8   Quoted by Dennis, pp. 114-15.

9   See, for example, Martyn Hammersely's interesting discussion of how a study by Peter Foster, which concluded there was no evidence of direct or indirect racism in a multi-ethnic inner city school which he studied, was rejected in mainstream sociology because it violated 'the widely accepted theoretical assumption that racism is institutionalised in British society' (*The Politics of Social Research*, Sage, 1995, p. 69). Empirical evidence cannot refute the claims of those who believe institutional racism is pervasive.

10 David G. Green, 'Inventing new crimes and suppressing free speech', in Alex Deane (ed.), *Big Brother Watch. The State of Civil Liberties in Modern Britain*, London: Biteback, 2010, p. 106.

11 Quoted in Dennis, p. xviii,

12 Munira Mirza, 'Rethinking race', *Prospect*, October 2010, p. 32.

13 Andrew Porter and Rebecca Smith, 'Age discrimination in NHS must end says Andy Burnham', *Daily Telegraph*, 21 October 2009.

14 Disability Discrimination Act, chapter 50, Part II.

15 David G. Green, *We're (Nearly) All Victims Now!*, Civitas, 2006, p. 58.

16 HM Government, *The Equality Strategy: building a fairer Britain*, December 2010, p. 15.

17 *The Equality Strategy*, p. 15.

18 Conservative MP Dominic Raab suggests that 'positive action' will in practice be indistinguishable from 'positive discrimination' ('Tick the double standards box now' *Sunday Times*, 30 January 2011). Raab quotes the Government Equalities Office as saying that 'some information or evidence will be required' to justify hiring people on social rather than meritocratic grounds, but 'it does not need to be sophisticated statistical data or research', it could refer to local, sectoral or national data (so you can take pick, according to the outcome you want), and it may even be based on 'discussion with workers or their representatives.'

19 Bob Fahy, 'Positive action under the Equality Act 2010, *Human Relations*, 18 February 2011.

20 *The Equality Strategy*, p. 15.

5: One Law for You, Another for Me

1 The following section draws on David Green, 'Inventing new crimes and suppressing free speech', in Alex Deane (ed.), *Big Brother Watch. The State of Civil Liberties in Modern Britain*, London: Biteback, 2010, pp. 94-112.

2 David G. Green, *We're (Nearly) All Victims Now!*, Civitas, 2006, p. 47.

3 Green, *We're (Nearly) All Victims Now!*, p. 52.

4 Quoted in Green, *We're (Nearly) All Victims Now!*, p. 9 (emphasis added).

5 Green, *We're (Nearly) All Victims Now!*, p. 5.

6 These and subsequent figures are from David Green, 'Inventing new crimes and suppressing free speech', in Alex Deane (ed.), *Big Brother Watch. The State of Civil Liberties in Modern Britain*, London: Biteback, 2010, pp. 94-112.

7 David G. Green, 'Inventing new crimes and suppressing free speech', in Alex Deane (ed.), *Big Brother Watch. The State of Civil Liberties in Modern Britain*, London: Biteback, 2010.

8 EHRC, *How Fair is Britain? Equality, Human Rights and Good Relations in 2010: The First Triennial Review*, 2010, p. 233.

9 *How Fair is Britain?*, p. 673.

10 *How Fair is Britain?*, Table 8.2.1.

11 HM Government, *The Equality Strategy: building a fairer Britain*, December 2010, p. 20.

12 Martin Beckford, 'Schools report 40,000 cases of racism a year', *Daily Telegraph*, 29 October 2009.

13 Adrian Hart, *Leave Those Kids Alone: how official hate speech regulation interferes in school life*, Manifesto Club, September 2011.

14 Beckford, 'Schools report 40,000 cases of racism a year'. At present, schools are only required to report 'racist incidents', although some also report what they consider to be cases of 'homophobia'. The last Labour government drafted a new

statutory duty on schools to record all 'prejudice-based abuse', classified by the nine protected identities set out in the 2010 Equality Act, but the Coalition government has yet to decide whether to implement this requirement (see Hart, *Leave Those Kids Alone*, chapter 2).

15 In 2009, the Christian owners of a Liverpool guest house were charged with a 'religiously aggravated' public order offence after telling a Muslim guest that Islamic dress codes for women were akin to 'bondage' and allegedly referring to Mohammed as a 'warlord' (John Bingham, 'Christian couple face losing hotel after criminal charges for offending Muslim woman', *Daily Telegraph*, 20 September 2009). In December, when the case came to court, the judge dismissed the charge on grounds of insufficient and inconsistent evidence (the defendants denied having referred to Mohammed as a warlord).

16 Green, *We're (Nearly) All Victims Now!*, p. 36.

17 J. S. Mill, *On Liberty*, Penguin 1982, p. 105.

18 'Fostering liberty', *Spectator*, 5 March 2011. The judiciary was similarly called upon to decide whether a black Pentecostal couple should be banned from fostering because of their views on homosexuality (even though they had been providing foster care for nearly twenty years with no complaints or problems). The judges decided in this latter case that Britain is a 'secular state', that Christianity forms no part of our Common law, and that the beliefs of Christian foster parents should therefore be subordinated to the diversity rules laid down by Derby City Council. The council suggested the couple might like to attend a 're-education programme (Tim Ross, 'Judges back fostering ban on "anti-gay" Christians', *Daily Telegraph*, 1 March 2011).

19 James Forsyth, 'One week to get a grip', *Spectator* 19 March 2011.

20 This is not the only example of Cameron's government having to live with the consequences of its timidity in Opposition. Its failure to oppose the child poverty targets in the 2010 Poverty Act has similarly bound it to policies which it does not believe in and cannot reasonably be expected to deliver. See Peter Saunders, 'Poverty of ambition: why we need a new approach to tackling child poverty', Policy Exchange *Research Note*, October 2009.

21 Quoted by James Forsyth, 'One week to get a grip', p. 13.

22 James Kirkup, 'Budget could break law on social inequality', *Daily Telegraph*, 26 August 2010.

23 Patrick Butler, 'Will the courts protect charities against the cuts?', 1 February 2011; http://www.guardian.co.uk/society/patrick-butler-cuts-blog/2011/feb/01/judge-quashes-grants-funding-cuts-decision

24 'Male pensioners could be £340 worse off a year under EU ruling', *Daily Telegraph*, 28 February 2011.

6: The Equalities Industry

1 www.iedp.org.uk. The Institute's inaugural Chair is Linda Bellos, a well-known left-wing activist and black lesbian campaigner. While researching this book, two approaches were made to the Institute asking how many members it had, but no reply was received.

2 A sample of jobs listed at diversitylink.co.uk on 4 May 2011.

3 For example, http://www.jobsite.co.uk/jobs/humanresourcesandtraining/diversityandequality

4 Quoted in J. Shackleton, *Should We Mind the Gap?*, Institute of Economic Affairs, 2008, p. 20.

5   HM Government, *The Equality Strategy: building a fairer Britain*, December 2010, p. 8.

6   Skills Funding Agency, *Single Equality Scheme Consultation*, Press release, 2 August 2010.

7   S. McGuire and M. Robertson, 'Assessing the potential impact of the introduction of age discrimination legislation in UK firms', *Proceedings of International Conference on Organizational Learning, Knowledge and Capability*, Ontario, 2007, p. 679. See also S. Lawrence, 'Some Facts about Ageism', *The Times*, 16 September 2004.

8   It looks less of a bargain if we assume that equalities legislation and monitoring will not deliver complete equality. The Impact Assessment on the 2010 Equality Act takes the £62 billion estimated cost of gender and ethnic inequality and assumes that the new law will reduce this by one-thousandth. It gives no rationale for this fraction, but in this game, we just make up numbers as we go along. This then produces a predicted 'benefit' of the 2010 Act amounting to £62 million per year. *Equality Impact Assessment*, p. 26.

9   Shackleton, *Should We Mind the Gap?*, p. 95.

10 EHRC, *Annual Report and Accounts*, 2008-2009.

11 EHRC, *Two Years Making Changes*, October 2009.

12 House of Commons Committee of Public Accounts, *Equality and Human Rights Commission: Fifteenth report of session 2009-10*, London: The Stationery Office, 22 February 2010. The report gives details of seven people who received a total of £629,000 in severance payments and were then paid another £338,000 in consultancy fees. Five of them moved to the new Commission with no break of service, and the report notes that 'they had good reason to expect before they accepted their severance packages that they would be re-engaged' (p. 13).

13 A consultant was paid £1,000 per day to take over the role and it took 18 months for the position to be filled. MPs complained the search for a new chief executive had been 'bungled' 'Equality watchdog's £1,000-a-day temp', *Daily Telegraph*, 27 June 2011.

14 Trevor Phillips, 'Foreword', *How Fair is Britain? Equality, Human Rights and Good Relations in 2010: The First Triennial Review*, EHRC, 2010, p. 7.

15 Anushka Asthana, 'Equality watchdog to lose half its budget', *The Times*, 4 February 2011.

16 Government Equalities Office *Resource Accounts 2009-2010*; http://www.equalities.gov.uk/pdf/GEO%20Resource%20Acc ounts%202009-10%20FOR%20WEBSITE.pdf

17 Frank Reeves (*Race Equality in Local Communities*, Birmingham, Waterhouse Consulting Group, second edn, 2007) reports that in 2004, race equality organisations were funded from seven sources: the CRE (20%), local councils (40%), other public authorities (10%), National Lottery (10%), regeneration funds (5%), own income generation (5%), and other (10%).

18 Reeves, *Race Equality in Local Communities*, ch. 2.

19 Reeves, *Race Equality in Local Communities*, p. 78.

20 Grampian Racial Equality Council, *Financial Review*, 2007-08.

21 http://www.lewisham.gov.uk/NR/rdonlyres/98540E87-0804-4FCF-A198-C24D98E4A783/0/e8b5301f460b405e8649268881674109item4 REALreport4thMarch2009.PDF

22 Plymouth and District Racial Equality Council, *Business Plan 2008-13*, August 2008.

23 Peterborough Racial Equality Council, *Annual Report and Accounts 2009-10*.

24 Oxfordshire Racial Equality Council, *Business Plan 2006-09*.

25 These statistics are from the *Equality Act Impact Assessment*, p. 35.

26 Institute for Government analysis of civil service headcount statistics, *Whitehall Monitor No.6*, 15 March 2011, Table 1.

27 House of Commons Written Answers (*Hansard*) 21 July 2010.

28 For example, Leicestershire CC has a 'Policy and Partnerships Team' based in the Chief Executive's office and consisting of a full-time manager on around £40,000 pa, a full-time Senior Policy Officer on around £35,000, and a half-time Policy Officer on around £25,000. Its equalities agenda was budgeted in 2009-10 at around £90,000 in all. Worcestershire CC spends considerably more — about £240,000 pa on its HR 'Diversity Team', and another £12,000 on staff diversity training. Devon CC says its 'corporate equality budget' is worth £80,000 pa. Northamptonshire CC has an Equality and Diversity Officer who is given a budget of around £40,000 for 'events.'

29 The Taxpayers Alliance, 'Council savings: Unnecessary jobs', *Research Note 77*, 12 October 2010.

30 UK quangos 2007, spreadsheet from: https://spreadsheets.google.com/ccc?key=tm4Dxoo0QtDrEO EC1FAJuUg#gid=0

31 'Yard spends £25m on citizen focus', *Daily Telegraph*, 19 May 2011.

32 'Outrage as police spend £450m on equality and diversity', London *Evening Standard*, 27 October 2006.

33 Office for Fair Access, *Annual Report and Accounts*, 2009-10.

34 'Olympics chiefs to hire ten equality managers', London *Evening Standard*, 1 August 2007.

35 Equality and Diversity Forum, *Annual Report* 2008-09.

36 Martin Beckford, 'Sex quiz for state workers scrapped', *Daily Telegraph*, 18 March 2011.

37 Predictably, the Impact Assessment for the Equality Act also claimed that the Act would produce counteracting 'benefits in the range of £101.6m to £133.6m.' However, as we have seen, claims like this should probably be taken with a pinch of salt—certainly, the Institute of Directors thought the benefits had been 'grossly exaggerated' ('IoD condemns government over £1 billion regulation bombshell', Institute of Directors press release, 19 January 2009, http://press.iod.com/2009/01/19/iod-condemns-government-over-1-billion-regulation-bombshell/).

38 Assume 220 working days per year. If eight days cost £30m, then 220 days cost (220/8)*30 = £586.7m. This estimate depends on the assumption that everyone involved in the eight day exercise is employed full-time in diversity monitoring, but some may have been deployed from other duties, in which case the total annual cost would be lower. On the other hand, not all existing diversity and equality staff may have been put on this work for these eight days, in which case the overall estimate should be higher.

39 Government Equalities Office, 'Equality Act 2010: The public sector equality duty: Reducing bureaucracy', *Policy Review Paper*, 17 March 2011.

40 *The Equality Strategy*, p. 9.

41 Forum of Private Business website, various news releases from June 2009.

42 'IoD condemns government over £1 billion regulation bombshell', Institute of Directors press release, 19 January 2009; http://press.iod.com/2009/01/19/iod-condemns-government-over-1-billion-regulation-bombshell/

43 British Chambers of Commerce, Business Policy Unit, 'Positive signs from government on reducing burden of red tape', 3 June 2010; http://www.britishchambers.org.uk/zones/policy/press-releases_1/positive-signs-from-government-on-reducing-burden-of-red-tape.html

44 Louisa Peacock, 'Gender pay gap to be disclosed by law', *Daily Telegraph*, 20 August 2010.

45 *The Equality Strategy*, p.14. British Chambers of Commerce estimates the cost of introducing gender pay reporting in 2013 at £1.4 million, with a recurring cost after that of £0.4 million per year (Business Policy Unit, 'Positive signs from government on reducing burden of red tape', 3 June 2010).

46 Lord Davies of Abersoch, *Women on Boards*, February 2011; http://www.bis.gov.uk/assets/biscore/business-law/docs/w/11-745-women-on-boards.pdf

47 *Women on Boards*, p. 7.

48 Elizabeth Harrin, 'Is Norway working?: The case for women on boards', *The Glass Hammer*, March 11 2010; http://www.theglasshammer.com/news/2010/03/11/is-norway-working-the-case-for-women-on-boards/. Norway introduced a voluntary quota for listed companies of 40% women directors in 2003, and this was made mandatory in 2006. The result was that a small number of high-flying women spread themselves across a large number of board seats (the so-called 'golden skirts'), and many companies had to resort to appointing young and inexperienced women to meet their quotas. Company performance dipped as a result.

49 Bojan Pancevski and James Ashton, 'EU tells firms to put women on the board', *Sunday Times*, 6 February 2011. Catherine Hakim points out, however, that quotas appear to be illegal under EU law— *Feminist Myths and Magic*

Medicine, Centre for Policy Studies, January 2011. The European Professional Women's Network claims women currently make up 12% of directors on Europe's biggest companies, and that the current rate of increase would lead to parity in 16 years (Matthew Lynn, 'Sister Act' *Spectator*, 26 February 2011, p. 17).

50 *Equality Act Impact Assessment*, Annex AB.

51 *Equality Act Impact Assessment*, p. 48.

52 Olmec *A Guide to Equality and Diversity in the Third Sector* 2008; http://www.olmec-ec.org.uk/documents/website%5CPublications%2FGuide%20to%20Equality%20and%20Diversity%20in%20the%20Third%20Sector.pdf

In 1993, it was ruled that caps on pay-outs were illegal under European law, and since then there has been no upper limit on the value of awards in discrimination cases. See Anthony Fincham, 'Let's not forget Mrs. Marshall's 10-year sex discrimination claim', *The Times*, 25 August 2011.

53 Shackleton, *Should we mind the gap?*, pp. 52-53.

54 Claire Ruckin, 'Government unveils controversial employment tribunal reforms', *Legalweek.com*, 27 January 2011.

55 Thomas Sowell, *Affirmative Action around the World*, Yale University Press, 2004, p. 20.

56 P. Dolton, D. O'Neill, O. Sweetman, 'Gender differences in the changing labor market', *The Journal of Human Resources*, vol. 31, 1996, pp. 549-65.

57 R. Wright and J. Ermisch, 'Gender discrimination in the British labour market', *The Economic Journal*, vol. 101, 1991, pp. 508-22.

58 S. Lissenburgh 'Gender discrimination in the labour market', *Research Discussion Paper* 3, Policy Studies Institute, 2000.

59 Lord Davies of Abersoch, *Women on Boards*, p.14 and Annex A and B.

60 The following cases are taken from Jonathan Petre and Chris Hastings, 'Equality madness' *Daily Mail*, 23 January 2011; and Heidi Blake, 'Millions are wasted on equality audits', *Daily Telegraph*, 24 January 2011.

7: Are Unequal Outcomes Always Unfair?

1 EHRC, *How Fair is Britain? Equality, Human Rights and Good Relations in 2010: The First Triennial Review*, 2010.

2 *How Fair is Britain?* p. 14. The list and the terminology reveal the strong influence of Amartyr Sen's 'capabilities framework'.

3 The following statistics are taken from EHRC, *How Fair is Britain?* Part II.

4 The belief that there are too many immigrants 'correlates with media coverage' (p. 33), and negative attitudes to gypsies and travellers are 'exacerbated by inaccurate media reporting' which falsely links gypsies to crime and presents 'the nomadic lifestyle' as a problem (p. 35).

5 *How Fair is Britain?*, p. 29.

6 *How Fair is Britain?*, p. 40.

7 *How Fair is Britain?*, p. 29.

8 'Where equality was once contested political ground, all three of the main political parties went into the last election with an explicit commitment to equality in some form' (*How Fair is Britain?*, p. 12).

9 *How Fair is Britain?*, p. 47. It describes 'concern for equality' as 'a mainstream attitude'.

10 *How Fair is Britain?*, p. 7.

11 *How Fair is Britain?*, p. 637.

12 Thomas Sowell, *Affirmative Action around the World*, Yale University Press, 2004.

13 We shall see in chapter 9 that average IQ levels are higher among middle-class than working-class children, and ability is the single most important factor explaining educational achievement. Of course class origins have some effect, but ability is much stronger. For a detailed examination of the evidence, see Peter Saunders, *Social Mobility Myths*, Civitas, 2010, chapter 4.

14 In 2010, the Audit Commission reported that Labour had allocated £21 billion to Primary Care Trusts to reduce 'the health gap' between middle-class and poor areas, but most of this money appears to have been wasted as the gap between the poor and the better-off has actually widened. The Commission's managing director said that it has rarely been clear what impact this money had on health outcomes, and concluded that 'progress has been disappointing' (*Public health has improved but inequalities remain despite billions of pounds invested*, Audit Commission Media Release, 11 March 2010). It seems likely that bad diet, smoking, lack of exercise and other such factors explain the 10% increase in the life expectancy gap between 2000 and 2010 (Steve Doughty, 'The wasted NHS billions', *Daily Mail*, 5 July 2010).

15 Put technically, if the between-groups variance in the characteristics and attributes relevant to the outcome in question is significantly greater than the within-groups variance, the result will be a statistically significant difference in the group means—and hence a 'problem' to be explained.

16 As we shall see in chapter 8, some researchers do attempt to 'decompose' group differences to take account of individual factors. Research on the 'gender pay gap', for example, may try to control for the fact that men tend to be more qualified and more experienced than women. But the default position in these models is still one that assumes that any unexplained difference must be due to discrimination, even though many individual variations are never included in the models.

17 For example: Steven Lukes, *Power: A Radical View*, MacMillan, 1975; Stewart Clegg, *Power Rule and Domination*, Routledge & Kegan Paul, 1975.

8: Unequal Labour Market Outcomes

1   M. Firth, 'Racial discrimination in the British labour market' *Industrial and Labor Relations Review*, vol. 34, 1981, pp. 265-72.

2   I. McManus, P. Richards, B. Winder, K. Sproston, V. Styles, 'Medical school applicants from ethnic minority groups', *British Medical Journal*, vol. 310, no. 6978, 1995, pp. 496-500.

3   M. Wood, J. Hales, S. Purdon, T. Serjesen, O. Hayllar, 'A test for racial discrimination in recruitment practice in British cities', Department of Work and Pensions, *Research Report*, no. 607, 2009.

4   Chartered Institute of Personnel Development and Chartered Management Institute, *Tackling Age Discrimination in the Workplace*, October 2005, p. 5.

5   Statistics from Communities and Local Government citizenship survey, July 2010; http://www.agediscrimination.info/Pages/ItemPage.aspx?Item=226

6 NATFHE Equality Unit, *Challenging age discrimination* (no date);
   http://www.ucu.org.uk/media/pdf/6/g/agediscrim_1.pdf

7 EHRC, *How Fair is Britain?*, p. 447. This figure rises to 10% for black Caribbean people.

8 M. Shields and S. Wheatley Price, 'Racial harassment, job satisfaction and intentions to quit', *Economica*, vol. 69, 2002, pp. 295-326.

9 Robert Verkaik, 'Thirty years on women still face discrimination in the workplace', *The Independent*, 29 December 2005.

10 Liam Creedon, 'Disabled endure shockingly high level of discrimination', *The Independent*, 14 April 2010.

11 D. Leslie, J. Lindlay, L. Thomas, 'Decline and fall: unemployment among Britain's non-white ethnic communities 1960-99', *Journal of the Royal Statistical Society*, Series A, vol. 164, 2001, pp. 371-87; Carol Foster, 'Ethnic minorities in the labour market', *Equal Opportunities Review*, No.165, Joseph Rowntree Foundation, 1 June 2007.

12 M. Stewart, 'Racial discrimination and occupational attainment in Britain', *The Economic Journal*, vol. 93, 1983, pp. 521-44.

13 One of these so-called 'decomposition studies' does recognise that some black and Pakistani groups may suffer lower employment and income levels than comparable white workers at least partly because of 'a taste for isolation, rather than just the consequence of discrimination' — D. Blackaby, D. Leslie, P. Murphy, N. O'Leary, 'Born in Britain: how are native ethnic minorities faring in the British labour market?', *Economic Letters*, vol. 88, 2005, p.375. But this cultural dimension is hard to measure and therefore does not get included in these models.

14 C. Li and B. Wearing, *Between Glass Ceilings: female non-executive directors in UK quoted companies*, University of Essex, Dept of Accounting Finance and Management, 2003, p. 2.

15 The author of a Hansard Commission report, *Women at the Top*, suggests the existence of 'an attitudinal barrier — the clubby culture' represents a 'firmly fixed' barrier to women entering top public sector jobs (David Hencke, 'Women still denied top public sector jobs', *Guardian*, 15 December 2000). Similarly, the former Equal Opportunities Commission blamed a 'male-dominated culture' for keeping women out of the professions (Polly Curtis, 'Six thousand women missing from boardrooms, politics and courts', *Guardian*, 5 January 2007).

16 I. McManus and K.Sproston, 'Women in hospital medicine in the UK', *Journal of Epidemiological Community Health*, 2000, vol. 54, pp. 10-16.

17 R. Simpson and Y. Altman, 'The time bounded glass ceiling and young women managers', *Journal of European Industrial Training*, vol. 24, 2000, pp. 190-98.

18 Equalities advocates continue to ignore evidence on trends. The *Observer*, for example, recently carried a report claiming that two-thirds of new doctors are women, but only 30% of consultants are women, so the 'glass ceiling' must be the explanation (Rachel Ellis, 'Female doctors fail to break through the glass ceiling', *Observer*, 22 August 2010). No attempt was made to look at female entry rates at the time when present-day consultants first became doctors.

19 Lord Davies of Abersoch, *Women on Boards*, February 2011, pp. 2 and 13; http://www.bis.gov.uk/assets/biscore/business-law/docs/w/11-745-women-on-boards.pdf

20 V. Singh, S.Vinnicombe, P. Johnson, 'Women directors on top UK boards', *Corporate Governance: an international review*, 2001, vol. 9, pp. 206–16.

21 The gender pay gap is calculated by dividing women's average pay by men's average pay, multiplying by 100 to express this as a ratio, and then subtracting this result from 100. The pay gap reported by the EHRC and the Office for National Statistics is based on full-time earnings. See Stephen Hicks and Jennifer Thomas, *Presentation of the Gender Pay Gap*, Office for National Statistics, 4 November 2009.

22 Office for National Statistics, 'Earnings: Full-time gender pay gap narrows', *Media release*, 9 December 2010. Note that this is very different from the 23% pay gap figure used by Women's Minister Harriet Harman during the House of Commons debate on the Equality Bill in 2009. Harman's figure was later described by the UK Statistics Authority as 'misleading' because it combined both full-time and part-time hourly pay rates. Part-time work tends to be paid at a lower rate, and many more women do part-time jobs, so Harman was able to achieve a much higher overall pay gap figure this way. But it is misleading because male part-timers are also paid much less than full-timers (indeed, male part-timers get 3.4% less on average than female part-timers). Harman's figure was therefore as much a reflection of the full-time/part-time 'gap' as the gender gap. She was warned of this before the speech, but she ignored it. See BBC News, 'Harman pay gap data misleading', 12 June 2009; 'Is Harriet Harman a liar or just stupid?'; http://www.utterzebu.com/blog/2009/11/06/is-harriet-harman-a-liar-or-just-stupid/

23 *How Fair is Britain?* p. 410. Two months after the EHRC report was published, the Office for National Statistics reported that the pay gap fell from 12.2% to 10.2% between 2009 and 2010 (Office for National Statistics, 'Earnings: Full-time gender pay gap narrows', 9 December 2010).

24 Quoted by Shackleton, *Should We Mind the Gap?*, p. 20.

25 Ros Micklem, 'Gender equality and the Equality and Human Rights Commission', *Public Policy and Administration*, vol. 24, 2009, pp. 213-14.

26 *How Fair is Britain?*, p. 337.

27 *How Fair is Britain?*, p. 340.

28 *How Fair is Britain?*, p. 425.

29 *How Fair is Britain?*, p. 667.

30 Although occupational segregation has often been blamed for the gender pay gap (women cluster in occupations which then attract lower pay rates), Catherine Hakim shows there is no evidence to support this. Even within the same occupation, men tend to earn more than women and to gravitate to the higher positions in greater numbers. See Catherine Hakim, *Feminist Myths and Magic Medicine*, Centre for Policy Studies, 2011, p. 20.

31 See, for example, Steven Pinker, *The Blank Slate*, Penguin 2002, chapter 18. I also discuss this issue more fully in *Social Mobility Myths*.

32 For example: Lucy Ward, 'Gender split still thrives at work', *Guardian*, 31 March 2005.

33 Hakim, *Feminist Myths and Magic Medicine*, p. 4.

34 Office for National Statistics, 'Earnings: Full-time gender pay gap narrows', 9 December 2010.

35 *How Fair is Britain?*, p. 412.

36 Catherine Hakim, *Key Issues in Women's Work*, Athlone Press, 1996.

37 Debra Leaker, 'The gender pay gap in the UK', *Economic and Labour Market Review*, vol. 2, April 2008, pp. 19-24.

38 The Davies report on women company directors (*Women on Boards* p. 16) finds that male and female graduate entry rates are similar, and this equality is maintained at junior management level, but women then start to fall behind at higher levels. It thinks this is due to lack of flexible working arrangements, difficulties in achieving a work-life balance, and disillusionment with career prospects. The possibility that it reflects women's preferences is never discussed.

39 Singh *et al*, 'Women directors on top UK boards', p. 214.

40 Reported in Jack Grimston, 'Nah, forget it: lack of drive keeps women out of top jobs', *Sunday Times*, 20 February 2011. A report by the Higher Education Statistics Agency similarly finds that women tend to go for entry-level positions after graduating, while men may risk waiting in the hope of getting something better paid — Polly Curtis, '£1000 gap between men and women's pay after graduation', *Guardian*, 6 November 2007.

41 Catherine Hakim, *Workstyle Choices in the 21st Century*, Oxford University Press, 2000.

42 Catherine Hakim, *Little Britons: financing childcare choice*, Policy Exchange, 2008, pp. 20-21.

43 Christina Odone, *What Women Want*, Centre for Policy Studies, 2009.

44 Catherine Hakim, *Women's Position in the Labour Market*, Paper to Economic Research Institute of Northern Ireland, 12 May 2004.

45 Peter Saunders, *Reforming the UK Family Tax and Benefits System*, Policy Exchange, 2009, p. 89.

46 See, for example, R. Wright and J. Ermisch, 'Gender discrimination in the British labour market: A reassessment', *The Economic Journal*, vol. 101, 1991, pp. 508-22.

47 The Office for National Statistics states: 'It is important to note that gender pay gap estimates presented in ONS statistical bulletins do not reveal the extent of the difference in pay for men and women undertaking comparable jobs. They are not a measure of the extent of non-compliance with equal pay legislation' (Stephen Hicks and Jennifer Thomas, *Presentation of the Gender Pay Gap* p. 6). Unfortunately, this warning is rarely heeded.

48 Shackleton, *Should we mind the gap?*, pp. 47-48.

49 S. Lissenburgh 'Gender discrimination in the labour market', *Research Discussion Paper* 3, Policy Studies Institute, 2000. It should be noted that the final model still explains less than half the variation in pay between men and women, even after all these factors are measured.

50 Lissenburgh 'Gender discrimination in the labour market', p. 15.

51 A. Chevalier, 'Education, occupation and career expectations: Determinants of the gender pay gap for UK graduates', *Oxford Bulletin of Economics and Statistics*, vol. 69, 2007, pp. 819-42.

52 Chevalier 'Education, occupation and career expectations', p. 840.

53 N. Meager and D. Hill, 'The labour market participation and employment of disabled people in the UK Institute of Employment Studies', *Working Paper* 1, 2005, p. 27.

54 M. Jones, 'Is there employment discrimination against the disabled?', *Economics Letters*, vol. 92, 2006, pp. 32-37.

55 For example: D. Leslie, J. Lindlay, L. Thomas, 'Decline and fall: Unemployment among Britain's non-white ethnic communities 1960-99', *Journal of the Royal Statistical Society*, Series A, vol. 164, 2001, pp. 371-87; TUC *Recession Report* no. 6, April 2009, http://www.tuc.org.uk/economy/tuc-16336-f0.pdf

56 A recent Joseph Rowntree Foundation report found that the 'earnings penalty' for ethnic minorities in Britain was only partly explained by their clustering in different kinds of occupations. It concluded from this that 'Labour market discrimination is apparently deep-rooted, widespread and persistent' (Ken Clark and Stephen Drinkwater, *Ethnic Minorities in the Labour Market*, Joseph Rowntree Foundation 2007, p. x).

57 D. Blackaby, D. Leslie, P. Murphy, N. O'Leary, 'Born in Britain: how are native ethnic minorities faring in the British labour market?', *Economic Letters*, vol. 88, 2005.

58 Shackleton, *Should we mind the gap?*, pp. 101-02.

9: Inequalities in Social Outcomes

1 See R. Jenkins, 'Intervening against "racial" disadvantage', *Comparative Education Review*, vol. 32, 1988, p. 2.

2 The 'attainment gap' between black Caribbean and white students (measured as the proportion of students achieving five or more good GCSE passes) fell between 2002 and 2009 from 20 to seven percentage points. The GCSE pass rate has improved every year since these exams were introduced in the late 1980s (the proportion of pupils achieving five or more passes at grades A-C has swollen from 40% in 1989 to 70% in 2009), so this narrowing should not surprise us. As Paul Bolton observes: 'Beyond a certain point, performance gaps for any large group of pupils will *have* to fall for national results to continue improving. When results plateau in a high performing group, the low performing group needs to catch up for an overall improvement'. (http://www.parliament.uk/briefingpapers/commons/lib/research/briefings/snsg-05526.pdf).

3 Black Labour MP Diane Abbott says: 'Teachers are failing black boys... black boys do not have to be too long out of

disposable nappies for some teachers to see them as a miniature gangster rapper', (quoted in Tony Sewell, 'Master class in victimhood', *Prospect*, October 2010, p. 33.

4 *How Fair Is Britain?*, p. 307.

5 Asian = 5 per 10,000 pupils; whites = 9 per 10,000. Exclusions were highest among black Caribbean (30 per 10,000) and Gypsy/Roma children (38 per 10,000). *How Fair Is Britain?*, pp. 312-13.

6 *How Fair Is Britain?*, p. 332.

7 *How Fair Is Britain?*, Figure 10.6.4.

8 *How Fair Is Britain?*, pp. 422, 427.

9 'Systemic bias does not necessarily arise out of malice on the part of any individual, it nonetheless has the effect of creating conditions which restrict opportunities for some groups and entrenching inequality' (*How Fair Is Britain?*, p. 19). The report prefers to talk of 'systemic bias' rather than 'institutional racism' because it applies to gender as well as ethnic differences.

10 *How Fair Is Britain?*, p. 447.

11 Former head of Ofsted, Mike Tomlinson, recently stated that Chinese, Indian and Bengali parents tend to place more importance on education than white (and by implication, black Caribbean) parents do, and this explains the different levels of educational achievement among different ethnic groups—see Julie Henry, 'Ethnic minority pupils race ahead of poor white classmates in schools', *Daily Telegraph*, 1 March 2009. See also: David G. Green, *We're (Nearly) All Victims Now!*, Civitas, 2006, pp. 68ff.

12 The following data are from R. Berthoud, 'Family formation in multi-cultural Britain', Institute for Social and Economic Research, *Working Paper* no. 34, 2000, University of Essex;

and Amanda White, *Social Focus in Brief: ethnicity*, London: Office for National Statistics, December 2002.

13 Tony Sewell, 'Master class in victimhood', *Prospect*, October 2010, p. 33.

14 Graeme Paton, '100 schools dominate Oxbridge admissions', *Daily Telegraph*, 20 September 2007.

15 Graeme Paton, 'Private school pupils dominate universities', *Daily Telegraph*, 6 October 2009.

16 The EHRC's fairness report, for example, includes as one of its main aims a reduction in the 'disparities in educational performance by socio-economic background', *How Fair Is Britain?*, p. 668.

17 Graeme Paton, 'Universities need quota of poor students', *Daily Telegraph*, 22 August 2010.

18 Jack Grimston, 'Oxford may cut private entrants', *Sunday Times*, 13 March 2011.

19 Peter Saunders, *Social Mobility Myths*, Civitas, 2010.

20 *Social Mobility Myths*.

21 Interestingly, the EHRC report notes that although 'ethnic differences in GCSE results have narrowed... the gap between students from different socio-economic backgrounds remains wide' (*How Fair Is Britain?*, p. 325). black Caribbean, Pakistani and Bangladeshi students all now perform as well on average as white British students. This pattern of ethnic convergence and social class persistence is exactly what we would predict if innate ability is driving success, for while there is no reason why ability levels should vary between ethnic groups (which means their outcomes should converge as opportunities improve), average ability continues to vary between classes (because in

each generation, classes tend to be recruited according to ability and talent).

22 *How Fair Is Britain?*, p. 81.

23 ONS press release, 2008, quoted in Christopher Snowdon, *The Spirit Level Delusion*, Little Dice, 2010, p. 93.

24 Research by Balarajan *et al*, published in the *British Medical Journal* on 18 March 1989, and cited by Snowdon, p. 95, fn. 25.

25 Snowdon, citing a research review in *The Lancet* by Robert Goldenberg, p. 91.

26 *How Fair Is Britain?*, p. 135.

27 Macpherson Report, quoted by P. Waddington, K. Stenson and D. Don, 'In proportion: race, and police stop and search', *British Journal of Criminology*, vol. 44, 2004, p. 889.

28 Waddington *et al*, 'In proportion', p. 909. Unfortunately, so ingrained is the belief in some kind of 'institutional racism' that the authors still speculate at the end of their paper that, although there is no evidence of the police deliberately or even unwittingly stopping more 'available' ethnic minority people than whites, the 'racial patterning of unemployment, homelessness and school exclusion' means that ethnic minorities spend more time in public places, which means they are more exposed to stop and search (p. 910). In other words, blacks are more likely to be unemployed or excluded from school, which means they are more likely to be observed by the police hanging around, and are therefore more prone to be stopped—and this difference in their 'availability' reflects 'institutional racism.' If you search long and hard enough, you will always find what you are looking for.

29 Of those stopped and searched in 2008/09, 9% of blacks were arrested compared with 10% of whites, 10% of Mixed Race people, and 8% of Asians—*How Fair Is Britain?*, p. 135.

30 *How Fair Is Britain?*, p. 171.

31 House of Commons, *Young Black People and the Criminal Justice System*, 2nd report of session 2006-0, vol.1.

32 *Young Black People and the Criminal Justice System*, pp. 28-29. Besides social exclusion, the other main factors contributing to black over-representation in the crime statistics were 'family patterns' (especially the lack of adult male role models in many black Caribbean families) and 'perceived and actual discrimination' (including police stop and search patterns, which are described as 'still a cause for concern', p. 45)

33 HM Government, *The Equality Strategy: building a fairer Britain*, December 2010, p. 21.

34 *The Equality Strategy*, pp. 6-7.

35 *The Equality Strategy*, p. 7.

36 EHRC, *How Fair Is Britain?*, Figure 9.1.4.

37 27% of Chinese men and 25% of Indian men are in professional jobs compared with 14% of white British men.

38 51% against 42%. This contrasts with just 28% of Pakistanis and Bangladeshis. *How Fair Is Britain?*, p. 60.

39 Asian = 5 per 10,000 pupils; whites = 9 per 10,000. Exclusions were highest among black Caribbean (30 per 10,000) and Gypsy/Roma children (38 per 10,000). *How Fair Is Britain?*, pp. 312-13 .

40 Proportions achieving five or more good GCSE passes including maths and English: Chinese 72%; Indian 67%;

Bangladeshi, white British and black African 51%; Pakistani 43%; black Caribbean 39% — *How Fair Is Britain?*, p. 332.

41 67% of white pupils say they were bullied between 2004 and 2006, compared with 62% of black Africans, 61% of black Caribbeans, 58% of Pakistanis, 52% of Bangladeshis and 49% of Indians — *How Fair Is Britain?*, p. 321. Violence is reported by 3% of whites and 2% of ethnic minority group members (p. 220).

42 49% of blacks and 45% of Asians felt able to influence decisions in their local area compared with 36% of whites — *How Fair Is Britain?*, p. 603.

43 'Systemic bias does not necessarily arise out of malice on the part of any individual, it nonetheless has the effect of creating conditions which restrict opportunities for some groups and entrenching inequality' *How Fair Is Britain?*, p. 19. The report prefers to talk of 'systemic bias' rather than 'institutional racism' because it applies to gender as well as ethnic differences.

44 'Asian students were also presented in seemingly benign terms as passive and studious and not presenting a disciplinary problem for teachers — a seemingly positive attribute. This notion of the 'passive Asian' student was juxtaposed against the 'aggressive' student of Caribbean origin and became... a stick to beat the West Indian pupil with... Here we see a form of institutional racism that exhibits seemingly positive attributes', Mike Cole, '"Brutal and stinking" and "difficult to handle": the historical and contemporary manifestations of racialisation, institutional racism and schooling in Britain', *Race Ethnicity and Education*, vol. 7, 2004, p. 45. Note that Cole makes no attempt to discover whether Asian students really are more studious and better-behaved — this judgement is automatically treated as a racist stereotype, so no further investigation is warranted.

45 John Carvel, 'Targets on the way to boost ethnic minority leadership in NHS', *Guardian*, 14 January 2009.

46 *How Fair Is Britain?*, p. 74.

47 In England, 32% of men are 'normal/healthy weight' compared with 42% of women—*How Fair Is Britain?*, p. 286.

48 Suicide rate for men = 17.7 per 100,000; women = 5.4 per 100,000—*How Fair Is Britain?*, p. 91.

49 *How Fair is Britain?*, Executive Summary, p. 13.

50 Only four of 129 fatalities at work in 2008/09 were women—*How Fair Is Britain?*, p. 639.

51 Men are three times more likely to be stopped and searched by the police—*How Fair Is Britain?*, p. 131.

52 *How Fair Is Britain?*, p. 164.

10: What Is To Be Done?

1   David G. Green, *We're (Nearly) All Victims Now!*, Civitas, 2006, p. 77.

2   See Carl Boggs, *Gramsci's Marxism*, Pluto Press, 1976; also Leszek Kolakowski, *Main Currents of Marxism, volume 3: The Breakdown*, Oxford University Press, 1981, chapter 6.

3   The term 'culture wars' was coined in the USA by James Davison Hunter in his 1991 publication, *Culture Wars: The Struggle to Define America*, Basic Books, 1992.

4   There is a parallel here with what Norman Dennis says about the role of the social affairs intellectuals in undermining support for marriage and the traditional family model (*Rising Crime and the Dismembered Family*, IEA Health and Welfare Unit, 1993; http://www.civitas.org.uk/pdf/cw18.pdf)

5   Even someone like Linda Bellos, a lifelong black lesbian activist and former leader of Lambeth Council in its 'loony-left' heyday in the 1980s, has now been given an OBE (in 2006) for 'services to diversity' (we saw earlier that she also heads the Institute of Equality and Diversity Practitioners). During her time in charge of Lambeth, Bellos banned the word 'family' from council literature because it was 'discriminatory', and stopped the police from using council facilities because they were, in her words, 'bent on war' (Paul Lindford, 'Where are they now?: Linda Bellos' http://www.totalpolitics.com/history/3888/where-are-they-now-linda-bellos.thtml). Her Wikipedia entry says of her decision to accept the OBE: 'She was reluctant to receive the award, due to the Honour's association with colonialism, but was encouraged to accept it by her family.' The Queen must have been delighted.

6   Neil O'Brien, 'Just deserts? Attitudes to fairness, poverty and welfare reform', Policy Exchange *Research Note*, April 2011. The survey finds the strongest support for a meritocratic conception of fairness ('In a fair society, people's incomes should depend on how hard they work and how talented they are': 85% agree, 8% disagree), and also records strong support for the free market, liberal proposition that: 'In a fair society, people's incomes should depend on how much other people value the services they provide' (63% agree, 24% disagree). The egalitarian end-state equality statement attracts the least support of the three. This pattern appears very stable over time, for I recorded very similar results when I used these three statements in a public opinion survey conducted 20 years ago (discussed in Peter Saunders, *Social Mobility Myths*, Civitas, 2010, p. 138).

7   Munira Mirza, 'Rethinking race', *Prospect*, October 2010, pp. 31-32.